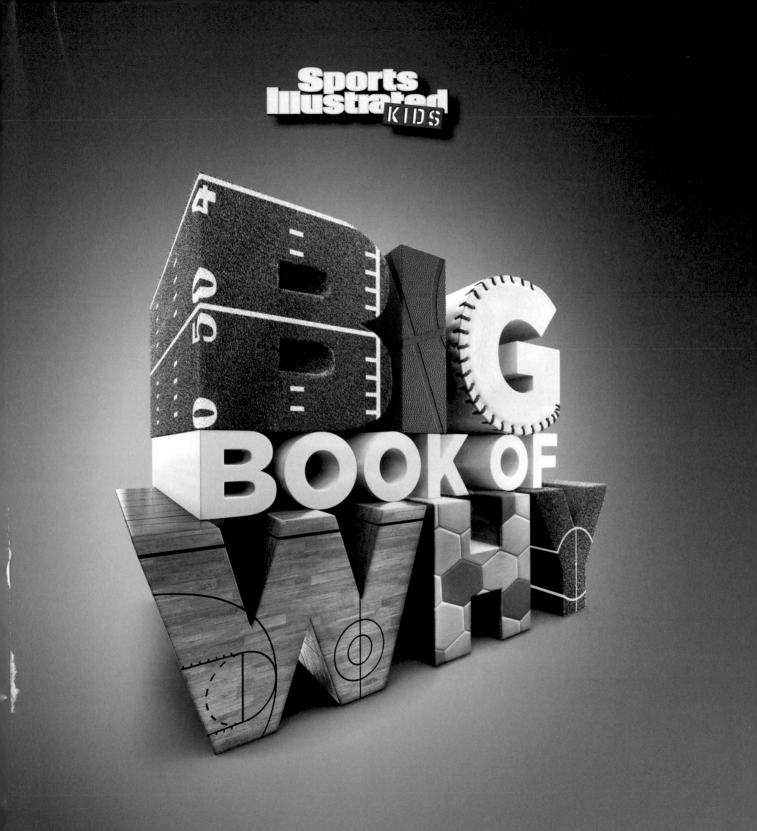

Sports Illustrated Kids

Managing Editor and Publisher Bob Der
Creative Director Beth Power Bugler
Project Editor Andrea Woo
Director of Photography Marguerite Schropp Lucarelli

Created by 10Ten Media

Managing Director Scott Gramling
Creative Director Ian Knowles
Project Editor / Writer Joseph Levit
Senior Writer Steven Bennett
Designer Elizabeth Flach
Assistant Editor Zachary Cohen
Reporter Corinne Cummings

ISBN: 978-1-61893-035-4
Library of Congress Control Number: 2012940486

First edition, 2012

5 QGT 17

10 9 8 7 6 5

To order Time Inc. Books Collector's Editions, please call (800) 327-6388,
Monday through Friday, 7 a.m.-9 p.m., Central Time.

We welcome your comments and suggestions about Time Inc. Books.
Please write to us at:
Time Inc. Books
Attention: Book Editors
P.O. Box 62310
Tampa, FL 33662-2310
(800) 765-6400

timeincbooks.com

Time Inc. Books products may be purchased for business or promotional use.
For information on bulk purchases, please contact Christi Crowley in the
Special Sales Department at (845) 895-9858.

Welcome

This book has all the questions . . . and the answers about the world of sports. It is divided into four chapters, each one containing questions that are more challenging than those in the prior chapter. At the end of each chapter is a quiz so that you can test what you've learned against the knowledge of an adult in your life who knows a lot about sports!

Contents

28

65

78

110

BIG LEAGUE QUESTIONS

Why aren't footballs perfectly round?

The first footballs *were* round, but because carrying the ball quickly became important in the early version of (American) football, the ball began to take on a shape similar to a rugby ball. The blunt ends of a rugby ball allowed carriers to tuck the ball into their arms more tightly. As the sport added more rules, like the number of downs and the amount of yards required to make a first down, passing the ball became more popular. And when the forward pass was made legal in 1906, the ball evolved to make passing easier, looking more and more like the football we know today.

DID YOU KNOW?
THE 1899 OFFICIAL FOOTBALL RULES DECLARED THAT A FOOTBALL SHALL HAVE THE SHAPE OF A "PROLATE SPHEROID"

Why do so many Brazilian soccer stars go by only one name?

In Brazil, calling people by their first name or nickname shows intimacy and familiarity. The public there particularly likes to call their top soccer players by only one name. One of the world's most famous soccer players was from Brazil. His full name is Edson Arantes do Nascimento. But he is better known as Pelé.

Why is Utah's basketball team called the Jazz?

If you're in Salt Lake City, Utah, and in the mood for jazz music, you're probably out of luck. But the nickname Jazz made sense in the team's original home city, which was New Orleans.

The New Orleans Jazz started as an American Basketball Association team in 1974. But things never went right in the Big Easy. They never had a suitable home court. They acquired former LSU star Pete Maravich, but couldn't figure out a way to win. They traded a Number 1 draft pick to the Lakers that would become NBA legend Magic Johnson. They drafted Hall of Famer Moses Malone, but gave up his rights.

Still, the ownership decided to keep the team name and colors when the franchise moved to Utah after just five seasons.

Why don't pitchers throw complete games all the time?

There are several reasons pitchers rarely throw complete games in modern baseball. Back in the day, bullpens were where managers kept the guys who couldn't cut it as starters. Managers didn't want to use bullpen pitchers if at all possible, so they kept their starters in as long as the game didn't get totally out of hand. These days, bullpens are stocked with good pitchers, so there is little reason for managers to rely on starting pitchers going the distance.

Since most hitters are stronger today, pitchers need to throw a lot more hard-breaking pitches. This puts a more strain on the elbow. So, pitchers are expected to last fewer innings than the nine of days past.

Finally, in an effort to protect the health of pitchers, teams now limit the number of pitches a starter will throw. Pitchers that go too long into games, or throw too many innings in a season, put themselves at a much greater risk of serious injury.

DID YOU KNOW?
ROY HALLADAY LED THE MAJORS IN COMPLETE GAMES SEVEN TIMES BETWEEN 2003 AND '11

Why don't PGA Tour golfers ever wear shorts?

Because the PGA Tour is serious about their dress code! Even when the temperature reaches 100 at a PGA tournament, you won't see a player wearing shorts. The PGA Tour dress code bans shorts, blue jeans, tank tops, and collarless shirts (though some tournaments do let players get away with no collar).

The lucky ones are the caddies. They're allowed to wear shorts as long as they're knee-length, not denim, and a solid color.

Why does Notre Dame wear gold helmets?

Notre Dame's campus in South Bend, Indiana, features a 187-foot tall structure called The Main Building. On top of The Main Building is a 19-foot-tall statue of Mary, the Mother of God, which is where the school gets its name (in French, Notre Dame means "Our Lady"). The statue stands atop a shining golden dome, which is why Irish football players are golden-domed themselves. The Irish program is so serious about matching their helmets to that dome that they mix 23.9-karat golden flakes from the dome itself into the helmet paint!

Why do bats splinter?

Not all wooden baseball bats are the same. For many years, most bats were made from ash trees. Ash bats chip or flake as they absorb a beating from high-speed pitches, so the barrel softens over time. A batter usually notices a crack forming in the bat before it becomes a serious issue. He can then switch to a fresh bat.

In 1997, the major leagues allowed players to use baseball bats made of maple for the first time. Many players like maple bats better because they are lighter, helping them swing more quickly. But maple bats don't flake or chip slowly over time. They appear to be unfazed on the outside. Yet inside, a crack can be growing. When maple bats break, they do so suddenly, and with a lot of wood flying around an infield or toward the crowd. Maple also has a tendency to explode at the point of contact in cold weather. MLB is considering phasing out maple bats, and going back to only ash.

Why is Stanford's mascot a tree?

Ask Stanford University that question, and the answer is simple: It isn't. Stanford University does not have a mascot!

The Stanford Tree is actually the mascot of the school's marching band. But as one of the country's unique (and very weird) mascots, The Tree gets a lot of attention when the Cardinal football or basketball teams are on TV.

You might be wondering why Stanford's mascot isn't a red bird. Well, they're not the *cardinals*; they're the *Cardinal*, as in a shade of the color red. But back to that big, goofy Tree. In 1975, the marching band tried out some new mascots. The contestants included a steaming manhole cover, a french fry, and a tree (obviously, it wasn't a very serious competition). The Tree was so popular with the crowd that they kept on bringing it back. Soon, The Tree started to feel a lot like the school's mascot.

The Tree isn't totally ridiculous. Stanford is located in Northern California, which is famous for giant redwood trees. In fact, El Palo Alto, a famous redwood in the nearby city of Palo Alto, is on the Stanford University seal.

DID YOU KNOW? STANFORD UNIVERSITY'S SPORTS TEAMS WERE KNOWN AS THE INDIANS FROM 1930 TO '72

Why are bumps on a trail called moguls?

The word we now know as "mogul" probably evolved from two other languages. The word *mug*, meaning "small hill," comes from a German dialect. The word *mugel*, which also means "small hill," is found in an Austrian dialect.

Skiers naturally form moguls when they begin to use some of the same pathways down a ski slope. Over time, snow gets pushed into mounds or piles.

DID YOU KNOW?
SOME SKI RESORTS CREATE MOGUL RUNS SO THAT PEOPLE CAN PRACTICE ON THEM

Why do some football and baseball players wear eye black?

When you're trying to hit a baseball or catch a football, eyesight is very important. And the glare from the sun on a clear day can be a tough obstacle to overcome.

In 1942, Washington Redskins fullback Andy Farkas smeared burned cork ashes under his eyes. He's known as the first football player to wear eye black. The idea behind eye black is that the dark substance will absorb the light, thereby reducing the sun's glare. Studies have shown that it reduces glare only a small amount, but athletes will do anything to gain even a slight edge.

Why does Ichiro wear his first name on his uniform?

Having the name Suzuki in Japan is kind of like having the name Smith or Jones in the U.S. In fact, Suzuki is the second-most-common last name in Japan.

During his first two years as a pro in the minors, Ichiro was often a bench warmer for the Orix BlueWave. Fortunately, new manager Akira Ogi was hired before Ichiro's third pro season. Ogi was so impressed by Ichiro's bat skills and speed that he named him the starting rightfielder. Ogi felt Ichiro was such a special player that he shouldn't be just another Suzuki. The team asked him to start wearing his first name on his jersey.

At first, Ichiro didn't like the extra attention. But he came to appreciate it later (maybe three MVP awards in Japan's Nippon Professional Baseball League helped). When he came to the U.S. in 2001, Major League Baseball let him wear "Ichiro" on the back of his Seattle Mariners jersey.

Long-time manager Dusty Baker once said: "Anybody that just goes by one name has got to be cool. Man, he's Ichiro. That says it all, doesn't it?"

DID YOU KNOW?
ICHIRO WAS THE SECOND-FASTEST MLB PLAYER TO REACH 2,000 HITS, AND THAT DID NOT INCLUDE HIS 1,278 HITS IN JAPAN

Why do Ohio State football players have little stickers on their helmets?

Those aren't just stickers, they're awards. When players or their units make a great play, the coaching staff awards them with a sticker. OSU's nickname is the Buckeyes, named after Ohio's state tree. So each sticker has a little picture of a Buckeye leaf.

Ohio State started using the stickers in 1968 under legendary coach Woody Hayes. They have become one of college football's great traditions — so much so that many other schools now also give out helmet stickers to players.

Why does the amount of splash affect a diver's score?

The splash created by a diver as he or she enters the water is one of the five parts of a dive that judges evaluate to determine an overall score. In order, a diver's judges score the approach, takeoff, elevation, execution, and entry. Because it is the last part of the dive that judges see, the entry leaves a strong impression on them. For this reason, divers are always trying to create as little splash as possible. An entry that creates little to no splash is called a rip entry. To attempt a rip entry, divers use one hand to hold the other hand in a position that will establish a flat surface when the diver hits the water. This technique creates some space at the water's surface for the diver to "fall through," creating less of a splash.

DID YOU KNOW? SYNCHRONIZED DIVING WAS ADDED TO THE OLYMPICS FOR THE 2000 GAMES IN SYDNEY, AUSTRALIA

Why isn't soccer more popular in the U.S.?

In many countries around the world, soccer is by far the most important sport. But by the time soccer came to this country, the people living here had already established their own sports. Baseball, American football, basketball, and hockey left little space for soccer to gain a foothold. It is also important to consider one of the main restrictions of soccer — that no player can use their hands except the goalie. Since all four of the major sports in the U.S. allow and even require athletes to use their hands, soccer may feel even more foreign here.

Why do hockey goalies wear a rectangle on their stick hand?

This part of a goalie's equipment, called a blocker, is just another way to prevent a goal from being scored. Instead of the glove goalies use to catch shots, the blocker allows goalies to bounce shots away from the net. Talented goalies are good at controlling the angle of the blocker. They can change the direction of a shot on goal, steering the puck to a teammate or at least away from players on the opposing team.

DID YOU KNOW?
MANY GOALIES HAVE THEIR MASKS PROFESSIONALLY AIRBRUSHED TO MAKE THEM UNIQUE WORKS OF ART

Why do swimmers wear skin-tight caps on their heads?

When swimmers glide through water, anything that is not streamlined and smooth will cause friction, which will slow them down. That is why swimmers shave off all of their body hair, and it is also why they wear skin-tight caps on their heads. They don't want their hair to cause any drag in the water. These days, swimmers sometimes even wear suits that copy the skin of dolphins and other fast-moving ocean animals. Less friction equals faster swimming.

Why did a team from Boise, Idaho, make a decision to move to a conference called the Big East?

The Boise State Broncos football team announced in 2012 that it would leave its conference to become part of the Big East conference. The Broncos were willing to compete two time zones away for two main reasons. First, the team makes more money as part of a more established conference. That means more scholarships for student athletes.

The second reason is respect. In 2004, '06, '08, and '09 the Broncos finished the regular season undefeated. Because they were from a smaller conference, they were never considered for the National Championship game. The Big East conference will provide a better chance.

Why are players on the Green Bay team called Packers?

When ex-high-school football rivals George Whitney Calhoun and Earl "Curly" Lambeau founded the team on August 11, 1919, they asked Lambeau's employer—the Indian Packing Company—for money to buy uniforms for the players. The company said it would provide the cash, but only if the team took on the company's name. So they did. In 1920, the Acme Packing Company bought the Indian Packing Company, and a year later the Packers were given a franchise in the new national pro football league. Today, the Green Bay Packers is the oldest team name still in use in the NFL.

DID YOU KNOW?

THE CITY OF GREEN BAY'S POPULATION OF LESS THAN 105,000 RESIDENTS MAKES IT ABOUT THREE TIMES SMALLER THAN THE NEXT-SMALLEST AMERICAN PRO SPORTS CITY

Why is a successful basketball shot worth two points instead of one?

When you put a shot into the net in soccer or hockey, your team gets one point. But when you swish a shot in basketball, you get two points. The reason why has everything to do with fouling.

Dr. James Naismith invented basketball in 1891. At first, scoring was simple: Make one basket, get one point. But Naismith soon realized that he needed to come up with a way to penalize teams whose players committed fouls. He experimented with a number of different rules. One of the early rules he came up with was awarding three points for a basket, and on a foul a team would get a free 20-foot shot that was worth the same three points.

Finally, in 1896, Naismith got it right. He settled on the basic system of two points for a field goal, and one for a free throw. And it would be another 37 years before basketball came up with the idea for the three-pointer.

Why is the fielder to the left of second base called a shortstop?

In the middle of the 19th century, baseball was not like it is today. Defensively, teams used up to 11 players. One infielder would cover each of the three bases. Everyone else scattered in the outfield. Baseballs back then were crummy and didn't weigh much. They couldn't be thrown very far. Doc Adams, a player for the New York Knickerbockers, started positioning himself between the outfielders and infielders. He would catch an outfielder's throw and relay the ball to the infield. The position was called the short fielder, or shortstop. The shortstop moved closer to the infield as the sport evolved, until the four infielders resembled the formation we see today.

DID YOU KNOW?
BEFORE 1858, ALL BASEBALLS WERE MADE BY THE PLAYERS THEMSELVES—WITH WHATEVER THEY COULD FIND TO BUILD THEM

Why did LeBron James change his uniform number from 23 to 6 when he joined the Miami Heat?

LeBron James wore uniform Number 23 for the Cleveland Cavaliers for the first seven seasons of his NBA career. In fact, he even wore 23 when he played for St. Vincent-St. Mary High School before he became a pro.

But even before he decided to leave Cleveland to sign with the Miami Heat as a free agent in the summer of 2010, he had decided to scrap Number 23 for Number 6.

He did this to honor his hero, Michael Jordan. Jordan, a six-time NBA champion with the Bulls and the most popular NBA player of all time, made the Number 23 iconic in the NBA. Jordan was a favorite of LeBron's and many players who have come into the league recently. LeBron once said that every NBA player who wears Number 23 should retire it and start wearing a new number.

LeBron ended up choosing 6 because it's the number he wore in practice and for the U.S. Olympic team.

DID YOU KNOW? MICHAEL JORDAN ONCE WORE NO. 12 WHEN HIS NO. 23 JERSEY WAS STOLEN JUST BEFORE A GAME

Why do NASCAR drivers wear long-sleeve suits when they drive?

Considering it's often well over 100 degrees inside a moving stock car, a lot of drivers would probably prefer a T-shirt and shorts. In fact, most drivers wear heat shields on the bottom of their shoes to keep their feet from feeling like they're burning up.

But those suits are worn for one very big reason: They're fire-resistant. If a driver's car catches fire, he or she won't.

DID YOU KNOW?
MOST DRIVERS WEAR FIRE-RESISTANT LONG UNDERWEAR DURING A RACE!

Why are some tennis players considered clay court specialists?

Of the three main surfaces in tennis (hardcourt, grass and clay), clay is the slowest. There's more friction between the ball and clay than there is with other surfaces. That causes balls to bounce higher and slower, leading to fewer winners and longer rallies.

Pure power players often dominate on faster courts like grass, where the ball barely bounces and instead flies past opponents. But clay, the surface used in the French Open, gives an advantage to players who use a more defensive style.

DID YOU KNOW?
RAFAEL NADAL'S SEVEN FRENCH OPEN SINGLES TITLES ARE MORE THAN ANY MALE PLAYER IN TENNIS HISTORY

21

Why has no one hit .400 since Ted Williams in 1941?

A player has hit .400 or better over a full season 28 times in Major League Baseball history. Yet no one has done it since 1941, when Boston Red Sox superstar Ted Williams hit .406. There have been some close calls since: San Diego Padres Hall of Famer Tony Gwynn hit .394 in 1994 and Kansas City Royals legend George Brett hit .390 in 1980. But since 2000, no one has hit higher than .372 in a season.

There are several factors working against a player being able to hit .400. First, there's the grueling travel schedule. Players today have to travel all over North America, battling jet lag when they change time zones. In 1941, Williams never had to travel farther west than St. Louis. Then there's the way bullpens are used today. Williams often faced the same pitcher four or five times in a game. Today, managers frequently bring in fresh arms late in a game. And against top hitters, they're sure to bring in "specialists," lefty relievers who get out lefthanded hitters, or righties who are extra-tough on righthanded batters.

There's also the fact that batting average is no longer considered the most important stat in baseball. Drawing a walk is considered by many to be just as good as a base hit, but it won't help a player's average. And in today's game, there's a much bigger emphasis on power hitting.

Maybe there will be another .400 season one day, but it's going to take a special kind of hitter.

Why does the NFL have so many rules against hitting quarterbacks?

There are two reasons that the NFL is protective of quarterbacks. First, there's the fact that when a quarterback is throwing a pass, he's in no position to protect himself. A ballcarrier can juke, duck, or lower his shoulder, but a quarterback throwing a pass is wide open for dangerous hits. Damaging hits to the head may lead to concussions. Those below the knee might result in major knee, ankle, or foot injuries.

Second, in the NFL the quarterback is by far the most important player. An injury to the quarterback can sink a team's entire season.

DID YOU KNOW?

THE SEASON-ENDING KNEE INJURY THAT TOM BRADY SUFFERED IN THE FIRST GAME OF THE 2008 SEASON LED TO A BAN ON HITTING QUARTERBACKS BELOW THE KNEE

Why doesn't college football have a playoff system?

College football is the only major professional or college sport that doesn't use a playoff system to determine its national champion, even though most fans favor such a system. As is so often the case when the majority of people are not being listened to, the lack of a college football playoff comes down to money.

Large schools in automatic qualifying conferences — which means that some of their schools are guaranteed to be in bowl games — make more money and have a better chance of competing for a national championship than teams that are not part of those conferences. So the coaches, athletic directors, and school presidents at those schools have no motivation to change the system. They aren't eager to level a playing field that currently helps them acquire top prospects and glory.

DID YOU KNOW? ALABAMA AND NOTRE DAME HAVE WON THE MOST NATIONAL TITLES SINCE THE START OF THE POLL ERA IN 1936, WITH NINE EACH

Why is it called a turkey when you get three straight strikes in bowling?

Bowling three strikes in a row used to be a lot harder than it is today. More than 100 years ago, on holidays like Christmas and Thanksgiving, owners of bowling alleys would sometimes give a live turkey as a prize to the first person on each team who got three strikes in a row. This strategy helped the owners get customers to bowl at their lanes, and it was a bonus for the talented or lucky bowlers.

Why is football called soccer in America?

In the late 19th century, the sport was called Association Football in the United States. It was only after World War II that people began to call it soccer in America. That name change probably happened in part because the sport was viewed by many people as foreign. But with the increasing popularity of American Football and the National Football League, there was also a need to differentiate the names of the two sports.

DID YOU KNOW?
PEOPLE IN ENGLAND CALLED THE SPORT "ASSOCCER" IN THE LATE 1800S

DID YOU KNOW?
PITTSBURGH PENGUINS CENTER SIDNEY CROSBY SCORED HIS FIRST NHL HAT TRICK WHEN HE WAS 19 YEARS OLD IN A GAME AGAINST PHILADELPHIA ON OCTOBER 28, 2006; CROSBY WOULD END THAT SEASON AS THE YOUNGEST SCORING CHAMPION EVER IN ANY MAJOR NORTH AMERICAN PROFESSIONAL SPORT

Why is it called a "hat trick" when a hockey player scores three goals in a game?

It wasn't originally a hockey term. Hat trick referred to a feat in cricket. In 1858, cricket bowler H.H. Stephenson took three wickets with consecutive balls. Everyone was so impressed that they took up a collection and actually bought him a hat as a reward.

Hockey has its own origin story for the hat trick. According to the Hockey Hall of Fame, in 1946 Chicago Blackhawk Alex Kaleta was shopping for a hat in a Toronto store but didn't have enough money to buy it.

The shop owner told him that he could have the hat for free if Kaleta scored three goals against the Toronto Maple Leafs in that night's game. Kaleta scored four. The shop owner kept his promise, and Kaleta had a new hat.

Since the 1950s, fans have traditionally thrown their hats onto the ice after a player scores three goals in a game. No one has drawn more hats than Wayne Gretzky, who holds the all-time record with 50 career hat tricks during regular-season play.

Why do the Detroit Lions and Dallas Cowboys always host a game on Thanksgiving?

The Lions started out in 1929 as the Portsmouth Spartans. When Detroit radio station owner George A. Richards bought the Spartans and moved them to Detroit in 1934, he was desperate to differentiate them from the very good Detroit Tigers baseball team of the time. So he changed the team name to Lions, and decided to promote the team by having them play a game on Thanksgiving. The Lions got to play the undefeated Bears, and the game was broadcast on 94 radio stations nationwide. Though the Lions lost the game, the team sold out their 26,000-seat stadium. Playing on Thanksgiving became a tradition, and the Lions have played on the national holiday ever since, except leading up to and during World War II.

The Cowboys came into the Thanksgiving picture later. They were an expansion team in 1960. By 1966, the NFL wanted to add a second game on Thanksgiving. Dallas general manager Tex Schramm saw the chance to boost the popularity of his team. However, he was worried about turning a profit. He supposedly got a guarantee from the league that the Cowboys would get to host future Thanksgiving games. The Cowboys have failed to play a game on Thanksgiving only twice since then.

DID YOU KNOW?
THE COWBOYS' FIRST THANKSGIVING DAY GAME IN 1966 WAS THE FIRST TIME THE TEAM DREW MORE THAN 80,000 FANS TO A HOME GAME

Why do baseball players sometimes "choke up" on the bat?

When a ballplayer wants to get more control of the bat, he may decide to choke up. This means that he moves his hands from where they normally rest against the knob at the lower end of the bat to a position farther toward the barrel end of the bat. This practice gives many ballplayers a better chance at making contact with the ball, although at the same time they are also sacrificing power.

Why do college basketball uniforms only have numerals between 0 and 5?

Think about it. You don't see anyone in college basketball wearing Number 6 to honor LeBron James, right?

It's not because there are no LeBron fans out there. It's because NCAA (and a lot of youth and high school leagues) ban the use of numerals 6 through 9 on uniforms. It's so referees can more easily communicate with the official scorer. If there's a foul on Number 53, the ref can signal it to the scorer by holding up five fingers on one hand and three on the other. If there was a Number 8, that might get confusing.

For a long time, a single 0 (but not double 0), 1, and 2 were also illegal, because referees so often have to put up one or two fingers to signal the number of foul shots awarded to a player.

DID YOU KNOW? DIKEMBE MUTOMBO WORE NUMBER 55 FOR GEORGETOWN AND ALL SIX NBA TEAMS HE PLAYED FOR

Why do hockey goalies wear different masks than regular skaters?

Because goaltenders have pucks flying their way, they need masks designed to deflect those pucks away. Goaltender masks have more bars across them, making them better able to withstand shots. The masks also prevent goaltenders from absorbing the full force of a direct hit from a puck.

DID YOU KNOW?
PUCKS CAN TRAVEL AT THE GOALIE AT SPEEDS FASTER THAN 100 MILES PER HOUR

DID YOU KNOW?
OLYMPIC TARGETS HAVE 10 RINGS; THE GOLD BULLSEYE IN THE CENTER IS WORTH 10 POINTS

Why is the middle of an archery target called a bullseye?

There's no way of knowing the exact origin, but it's probably not because the target is the same size as a bull's eye. According to the Encyclopedia of Word and Phrase Origins, traditional bulleye targets were most often associated with rifle competitions in the U.K. In the early 19th century, there was a coin worth a crown that was nicknamed a bullseye (possibly because it was used to bet on barbaric bull-baiting contests, which have since been outlawed). And that coin was about the size of the middle of the target for those shooting competitions.

Why do gymnasts chalk their hands?

Gymnasts put chalk on their hands to create a strong and reliable grip. The chalk helps absorb sweat so the gymnast will be less likely to slip off of equipment such as the pommel horse, rings, or bars. Gymnasts will even put chalk on their legs to help during events like the high bar, uneven bars, and parallel bars.

The chalk is a powder called magnesium carbonate. It is not like the kind of chalk children use to draw on sidewalks. It is also different from baby powder. Baby powder also absorbs sweat, but it would decrease the friction between the bar and a gymnast's hands, leading to a weaker grip.

Why is a basketball team in Los Angeles called the Lakers when L.A. isn't known for its lakes?

When you think of Southern California, you think Hollywood and sunshine. But lakes certainly don't come to mind. So why is the famous basketball team from Los Angeles named the Lakers?

Simple. Originally, the team played in Minneapolis, Minnesota. And one of Minnesota's nicknames is the "Land of 10,000 Lakes." When the team moved west, they simply kept the name. And they had good reason to. During their 12 seasons in Minneapolis, the Lakers won five NBA titles!

DID YOU KNOW?
THE LAKERS HAVE WON 11 NBA TITLES SINCE MOVING TO L.A.

Why are Major League Baseball bats wooden instead of aluminum?

Balls hit by aluminum bats travel faster and farther than those hit by wooden bats with the same swing speed. In the major leagues, if hitters used an aluminum bat there would be a much greater risk of injury to opposing pitchers, especially in the case of a line drive toward the pitcher's head.

Why did the NFL recently change its overtime rules?

Pro football made a change to its overtime rules to make them fair. In the past, the first team to score in overtime would win, regardless of how they scored. That practice favored the team that was lucky enough to win the coin toss. That's because it was relatively easy for teams to produce a short drive and then kick a field goal for the win.

With the new rules, the team that receives the ball first in overtime wins if they score a touchdown on their first drive. If that team makes a field goal on their first drive, the opposing team gets a chance to run plays. If the second team doesn't score, the first team's field goal becomes the game-winner. Should the second team score a touchdown, they win. And should they kick a field goal to tie the game, the game's next score becomes the game-winner. This change makes the overtime more fair for both teams.

DID YOU KNOW? EVERY MOTHER'S DAY, HUNDREDS OF MLB PLAYERS USE PINK BATS STAMPED WITH A BREAST CANCER AWARENESS LOGO

Why are some dunks called alley-oops?

Surely everyone is familiar with basketball's alley-oop, when one player lobs a pass near the rim and his teammate grabs it and slams it in. The term comes from *allez-hop*, which is French for "Let's go." It's what French circus acrobats and trapeze artists yell as a cue to their partners when they are about to launch into the air.

"Alley-oop" actually started as a football term. In the 1950s, the San Francisco 49ers frequently had quarterback Y.A. Tittle lob high-arching passes to 6'3" receiver R.C. Owens, who simply out-leapt smaller defenders for easy catches. Alley-oops first popped up in college basketball in the 1960s, and slowly gained popularity. Now NBA players complete them all the time.

Why do baseball managers have to wear uniforms when coaches in other sports don't?

Even before they had to, most managers did wear their team's uniform. That's because in the early days of baseball a lot of mangers were also players. But for a long time managers who weren't also players didn't have to wear a uniform. In fact, Connie Mack, a Hall of Fame manager who led the Philadelphia Athletics from 1901 to '50, wore a suit to games. So did Burt Shotton, who managed the Philadelphia Phillies and Brooklyn Dodgers in the 1940s. Many managers felt that, since they were on the field for things like pitching changes, they should be dressed like the rest of the team.

In 1957, Major League Baseball put Rule 1.11(a) on the books: "All members of the team must wear a similar uniform." A manager might be able to challenge that rule, arguing that he's not a traditional member of the team. But seeing a manager in a nice dress suit would look very weird. Longtime Atlanta Braves manager Bobby Cox put it best: "Could you imagine going out there in shiny dress shoes? How would you kick dirt on the umpire?"

DID YOU KNOW?

BASEBALL'S FIRST UMPIRES WORE TAILED COATS AND TOP HATS

QUIZ TIME

Has reading this section made you a Big League sports fan? Find an adult who knows a lot about sports and see if he or she knows as much as you!

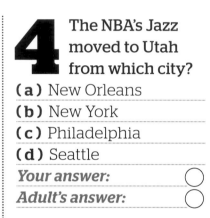

1 Edson Arantes do Nascimento is the full name of which all-time soccer great?
(a) Kaká
(b) Pelé
(c) Ronaldinho
(d) Ronaldo
Your answer: ○
Adult's answer: ○

2 For the first time in 1997, Major League Baseball allowed its players to use baseball bats made of which kind of wood?
(a) birch
(b) maple
(c) oak
(d) pine
Your answer: ○
Adult's answer: ○

3 Andy Farkas is known as the first football player to wear eye black when, in 1942, he smeared burned cork ashes under his eyes. Which NFL team was Farkas playing for at the time?
(a) Chicago Bears
(b) Green Bay Packers
(c) New York Giants
(d) Washington Redskins
Your answer: ○
Adult's answer: ○

4 The NBA's Jazz moved to Utah from which city?
(a) New Orleans
(b) New York
(c) Philadelphia
(d) Seattle
Your answer: ○
Adult's answer: ○

5 Which of the following was *not* among the contestants at Stanford University's marching band's 1975 tryouts for new mascots?
(a) a flying squirrel
(b) a french fry
(c) a steaming manhole cover
(d) a tree
Your answer: ○
Adult's answer: ○

6 Which Chicago Bulls jersey number did Michael Jordan wear for one game after his No. 23 jersey was stolen just before a game?

(a) 6
(b) 12
(c) 24
(d) 32

Your answer: ◯
Adult's answer: ◯

7 What was Kansas City Royals legend George Brett's batting average in 1980?

(a) .370
(b) .380
(c) .390
(d) .400

Your answer: ◯
Adult's answer: ◯

8 How many points is the gold bullseye in the center of an Olympic archery target worth?

(a) 10
(b) 20
(c) 50
(d) 100

Your answer: ◯
Adult's answer: ◯

9 The word we now know as "mogul" probably evolved from which two other languages?

(a) Austrian and German
(b) French and Polish
(c) Greek and Italian
(d) Romanian and Russian

Your answer: ◯
Adult's answer: ◯

10 Wayne Gretzky holds the NHL's all-time record for career regular-season hat tricks with how many?

(a) 20
(b) 30
(c) 40
(d) 50

Your answer: ◯
Adult's answer: ◯

ANSWERS:

(1 = b) (2 = b) (3 = d) (4 = a) (5 = a) (6 = b) (7 = c) (8 = a) (9 = a) (10 = d)

Your Total Score: ◯ | **Adult's Total Score:** ◯

LEVEL 1 ② 3 4

ALL-STAR QUESTIONS

Why is the NHL's championship trophy called the Stanley Cup?

It's named after Lord Stanley of Preston, who was the Governor General of Canada in the late 1800s. Stanley, who was from England, became a big fan of hockey after seeing it for the first time at a carnival in Montreal in 1889. His family became involved in the sport, and Stanley decided a challenge cup should be given to the best amateur team in Canada.

In 1892, he bought a decorative punch bowl and engraved "Dominion Hockey Challenge Cup" and "From Stanley of Preston" on it. Unfortunately, Stanley's term as governor was cut short. He left Canada in July 1893, and never saw the Cup awarded.

DID YOU KNOW?
NHL CHAMPIONS DON'T GET A NEW TROPHY. THEY HOLD THE STANLEY CUP FOR A YEAR, THEN TURN THE SAME CUP OVER TO THE NEW CHAMPS

Why are the Olympics held only every four years?

This four-year period of time, called an Olympiad, was the result of a peace agreement in ancient Greece between rival city-states Elis and Pisa. The Greek calendar was also based off of this length of time, and so the games — beginning in 776 BC — were always held four years apart.

Why is the San Francisco Giants' mascot a seal?

The Seal actually is *not* the Giants' first mascot. In 1984, the Giants introduced baseball's first anti-mascot: Crazy Crab. Fans were supposed to boo Crazy Crab, and the team even taped a commercial of manager Frank Robinson being restrained while trying to beat him up. The joke went a little too far though, with fans beaning Crazy Crab with anything they could get their hands on. He was retired after one season.

In 1996, the Giants rolled out Lou Seal. The animal was chosen for two reasons. First, there are real seals that pop up at Fisherman's Wharf in San Francisco. And second, there's the city's original team, the San Francisco Seals, who played minor league ball in the city from 1903 to '57.

Why is a standard marathon exactly 26.2 miles?

In 490 B.C., the Greeks faced a much larger Persian army on a battlefield near the town of Marathon in Greece. Wisely, they sent one of their soldiers (a professional runner) to Sparta to ask for help in fighting the Persians. The soldier, Pheidippides, had to run about 140 miles to deliver this request. The Spartans agreed to help, but for religious reasons would not do so until the next full moon. So Pheidippides had to run another 140 miles to deliver the disappointing news.

The Greeks, including Pheidippides, soon launched a successful surprise attack on the Persians. The Greeks killed 6,400 Persians, but lost only 192 of their own soldiers! The next part is likely myth — Pheidippides was supposedly asked to relay news of the major victory to Athens (about 25 miles away). He arrived, shouted either "Victory" or "Rejoice, we conquer," and then died of exhaustion. By 1896, organizers of the modern Olympic games in Greece commemorated Pheidippides' amazing sacrifice by holding a 25-mile race.

You can blame royalty for the extra 1.2 miles. The 1908 Olympics were held in London, England. Because the royal family wanted the race to end where they had set up viewing boxes, the race was extended. The distance became 26.2 miles; 13 years later, the International Amateur Athletic Federation made that the official length of a marathon.

DID YOU KNOW?
TOP AMERICAN MARATHONER MEB KEFLEZIGHI WAS BORN IN THE AFRICAN NATION OF ERITREA; HE BECAME A U.S. CITIZEN IN 1998, WHEN HE WAS 23

Why do tennis players have to wear white at Wimbledon?

Traditionally, tennis players wear white. And tradition is of the utmost importance at Wimbledon, which is the sport's oldest tournament. It has been held at London's All England Club since 1877.

In 1963, the All England Club said dress would have to be "predominantly white." In 1995, it was amended to "almost entirely in white." Penalties for improper clothing choices are left up to the referee, but the guidelines make it clear that players should not wear fluorescent or bold coloring. Pastels are preferred, and a player's shoes, socks, wristbands, and hat (or hairband) should also be white.

DID YOU KNOW?

WIMBLEDON IS THE ONLY MAJOR EVENT IN TENNIS THAT IS STILL PLAYED ON GRASS, THE SPORT'S ORIGINAL SURFACE

What exactly is a Cover-2 defensive scheme?

Versions of the Cover-2 defense — in which a team's safeties divide deep coverage responsibilities between them — have been around for a long time in professional football. It remains a key part of many defensive playbooks because it comes in handy during certain circumstances in a game.

When two safeties are used, this coverage divides the field up into halves. Each safety drops into a zone on his own side of the field, providing deep help for the outside cornerback. The cornerbacks and linebackers are each responsible for one of five zones covering shorter passes.

A Cover-2 defense typically limits big plays. It is designed to force the opposing offense to try to score points by executing long, mistake-free drives down the field.

DID YOU KNOW?
COACH TONY DUNGY'S "TAMPA 2" VARIATION OF THE COVER-2 HELPED MAKE THE BUCS' DEFENSE ONE OF THE NFL'S BEST

Why do drivers need to make pit stops during NASCAR races?

No, it's not a bathroom break. Drivers' cars need basic maintenance over the course of a race that's hundreds of miles long. In NASCAR, seven pit crew members are allowed over the wall and onto pit lane during a stop. Duties include changing all four tires and filling the tank with gas — which they do in just 13 to 15 seconds. In Formula One racing, cars are not allowed to refuel during the race. Pit stops are to change tires, which is finished in less than three seconds!

Why do baseball coaches encourage a level swing?

Many coaches believe a level swing has a better chance of creating backspin, which makes the ball carry farther. Bats swung evenly also make contact with the ball more often.

DID YOU KNOW?
ON MAY 13, 2012, REDS SLUGGER JOEY VOTTO BECAME THE FIRST PLAYER WHOSE THREE HOMERS IN ONE GAME INCLUDED A WALK-OFF GRAND SLAM

Why do cyclists usually ride in packs, rather than trying to out-race each other?

They actually *are* trying to out-race each other, but they're also all using each other to go faster. Racing in a pack, called a peloton, causes there to be less drag, or wind-resistance. Essentially, if you're riding right behind another bike, the bike in front of you is clearing a path of air for you.

There's strategy involved too. Members of the same team will often ride together in a peloton. And if a rider breaks away from the pack and takes a lead, his teammates back in the peloton will often slow down to prevent a competitor from being able to catch him. Teams also often have one rider known as a sprinter. Toward the end of a race, the sprinter's teammates will form a sort of mini-peloton to help the sprinter build up speed for a final push.

Why do players always stretch before games?

When people bend over to stretch their back or flex their legs and arms before beginning physical activities, they are engaged in static stretching. They make these motions because they believe it will prevent sore muscles, and keep ligaments and tendons from becoming over-strained. Studies have shown that this type of stretching does not offer a benefit compared to not stretching at all. In fact, in some cases, static stretching can actually be responsible for pulling muscles — the very thing people are trying to avoid!

Experts recommend dynamic stretching instead, which consists of warming up for an activity by slowly working your way into the motions used during the activity. For example, football or baseball players might start throwing a ball at short distances to each other, working their way up to the longer throws they will use in the game that put greater pressures on muscles and joints.

**DID YOU KNOW?
PITCHERS GENERATE SPEED AND POWER BY UTILIZING ENERGY FROM THEIR LEGS**

Why is it a bad idea to 'toe' a shot in soccer?

Though it may be easier to "toe" a soccer shot than to strike the ball on the laces, it isn't the best way to take a shot. When a player uses only the big toe to guide the ball, he or she has less control of where the ball ends up. It is a simple matter of surface area. By kicking the ball with the full foot, a player has more contact with the ball. Therefore, it is easier to place the shot just where it should go, and with greater power.

DID YOU KNOW?
DAVID BECKHAM IS ABLE TO BEND KICKS BY USING HIS INSTEP TO CREATE SPIN

Why don't NBA players wear T-shirts under jerseys like some college players do?

The NBA simply doesn't allow it. Under the Player/Team Conduct and Dress section of the NBA rulebook, number 4 of Section H reads: "While playing, players must keep their uniform shirts tucked into their pants, and no T-shirts are allowed." Many players wear protective padding under their jersey, but it's not permitted to be visible.

Why is the football field sometimes called the gridiron?

When the game was created, the football field had lines that ran vertically down the field, as well as the white horizontal markings that indicate yardage in the current version of the game. The intersecting lines made the field into a grid.

A more obscure possibility is that the field is a place to be closely inspected. The nautical dictionary says a "gridiron" is an "openwork frame on which vessels are placed for examination and repairs." Therefore, the men on the football field were being continually evaluated, and replaced when they were not executing plays as they should.

Why don't sprinters dive across the finish line?

Diving across the finish line doesn't help win the race. In track and field, the race is completed when the runner's torso (not the head, neck, arms, hands, legs, or feet) passes the finish line. So runners can dive head-first with arms out like Superman, but they wouldn't be considered across the finish line until the top of the chest crosses. That's why you often see sprinters lunge with their chests out as they approach the finish line.

DID YOU KNOW?
JAMAICA'S USAIN BOLT SET A WORLD RECORD IN 2009 WHEN HE RAN 100 METERS IN 9.58 SECONDS

Why is Number 42 retired in every Major League ballpark?

I n 1997, Major League Baseball retired the Number 42 for all teams in honor of Hall of Famer Jackie Robinson. Players who were wearing Number 42 at the time were allowed to continue wearing it. New York Yankees relief pitcher Mariano Rivera will end his career as the last Major League Baseball player to wear Number 42.

Fifty years earlier, in 1947, Robinson broke Major League Baseball's color barrier, becoming the first black player in MLB. Along with being a remarkably talented player, Robinson was a very brave one. In the 1940s, many felt that baseball should still be segregated, with black players playing only in the Negro Leagues. Robinson endured many taunts and threats, but the Hall of Famer is now considered a hero and a pioneer. Since his 42 was retired, no new players have been allowed to choose the number.

DID YOU KNOW?
SINCE 2009, ALL UNIFORMED PLAYERS, MANAGERS, COACHES, AND UMPIRES HAVE WORN NUMBER 42 IN ALL GAMES PLAYED ON APRIL 15, WHICH IS KNOWN AS "JACKIE ROBINSON DAY"

Why do some people call the badminton shuttlecock a birdie?

B ecause it traditionally has real feathers splayed out from one end, the shuttlecock has a higher drag than the balls used in other racquet sports. This drag causes the shuttlecock to decelerate rapidly after being hit, giving it the ability to fly a short distance and then float for a moment in the air, much like a bird in the moment between wing beats.

Why does the Tour de France leader wear yellow?

The history of the Tour de France's yellow jersey is a bit mysterious. The race leader used to wear a green arm band. Philippe Thys, a legendary rider from Belgium who won the Tour in 1913, '14 and '20, said race organizers offered him the yellow jersey in 1913. He didn't wear it though, because he thought he'd be too visible to competing riders.

So no one knew of the yellow jersey until 1919. Eugene Christophe of France wore it when he had the lead that year. But why yellow? One explanation is that it was in honor of race organizer *L'Auto*, a French newspaper that was famous for being printed on yellow paper. But an alternate explanation offered in *A Race For Madmen* claims that the race organizers needed enough jerseys to be able to supply the race leader with a new jersey each day, and that the supplier only had enough jerseys for the job in yellow, his least popular color.

Back then, Christophe hated wearing the yellow jersey. Spectators and competitors called him a canary. Now, the yellow jersey is what every road cyclist dreams of wearing.

DID YOU KNOW?
THE GREEN JERSEY IN THE TOUR DE FRANCE INDICATES THE RIDER WHO IS THE SPRINT CHAMPION

Why do skateboarders compete in a half-pipe?

In 1975, a group of skaters from California started going to Arizona to skateboard in giant water pipes being built there to divert water from the Colorado River to the city of Phoenix. But that was a long way to go to get their kicks and try out new tricks. So skater Tom Stewart and his architect brother Mike Stewart built the first half-pipe in their front yard in Encinitas, California. It allowed them to do trick after trick, and was featured in *Skateboarder* magazine. It quickly became the hotspot for skateboarders everywhere.

Why do the Montreal Canadiens have an 'H' in their logo?

The H stands for, what else, hockey. Early Canadiens logos involved the C, and from 1913 to '16 it was like today's logo, but with an A instead of an H inside the C (they were known as the Canadian Athletic Club). For the 1916-17 season, they changed the team name to Club de Hockey Canadien and moved the H inside the C. They've made some tweaks, but the H inside the C has been the basic logo for more than 80 years.

DID YOU KNOW?
THE CANADIENS' JERSEY ONCE FEATURED A MAPLE LEAF

Why is college football's biggest individual award named the Heisman Trophy?

It's named after John Heisman, a college football, basketball, and baseball player and coach at several colleges in the late 1800s and early 1900s. He was an innovator who helped bring the forward pass and center snap to football.

Heisman was the director of the Downtown Athletic Club in New York City, which in 1935 started giving an award to the best football player east of the Mississippi River. One year later, Heisman passed away and the Club named the trophy in his honor. The award now goes to the best college player in the country.

DID YOU KNOW?
THE TROPHY IS MODELED AFTER ED SMITH, A NEW YORK UNIVERSITY RUNNING BACK FROM 1933 TO '35

Why is "Take Me Out to the Ballgame" sung during the seventh-inning stretch?

In the early 1900s, successful entertainer and songwriter Jack Norworth was riding on a New York City subway. He saw a sign that said "Baseball Today — Polo Grounds." He was inspired to dash off a quick song about baseball. Fifteen minutes later, he had written "Take Me Out to the Ballgame." He worked with friend Albert von Tilzer, a Broadway songwriter, to put music behind the lyrics. The song was copyrighted in 1908, and both men promoted it. Many singers and actors started performing it during their acts. This made the song popular to the masses.

By the 1970s, famous broadcaster Harry Caray was singing it with fans of the Chicago White Sox at Comiskey Park. The team's owner gave Caray a microphone and he began to sing the song during the seventh-inning stretch. When Caray moved to Wrigley Field to announce Cubs games, he brought the tradition with him.

DID YOU KNOW? BROADCASTER HARRY CARAY SANG WITH CHICAGO CUBS FANS FOR 17 YEARS

Why is the home of the Boston Red Sox named Fenway Park?

Unlike most ballparks, Fenway isn't named after a team, person, or corporation. In 1911, team owner John I. Taylor bought land in Boston's Fenway neighborhood, and named his new ballpark after that location. But how did the Fenway neighborhood get its name? Before it was developed in the 1870s, it was a marshland. And fen is another word for a low, marshy area of land. And it didn't hurt that Taylor's family owned the Fenway Realty Company.

EMC LEVEL

ML.COM/KNOWS

Why is it so hard for national champions to repeat in men's college basketball?

S ince 1973, the NCAA tournament men's champion has won the next season only twice (Duke in 1992 and '93, and Florida in 2006 and '07). There are several reasons why it's so hard to repeat. First, teams that win the title usually have some very good players. And very good players often leave for the NBA as soon as they can.

Second, there's the three-point shot, which the NCAA adopted in 1986. During UCLA's dominance in the 1960s and '70s, stars Bill Walton and Lew Alcindor were simply too big to be stopped, and their lay-ups were worth just as much as any shot. Now, a less talented team can ride a hot three-point shooter to an upset win.

Third, there's the tournament itself. Teams have to win six straight games (some against other elite teams) to be crowned champion. Unlike in the NBA, if they lose even once, their season is over.

DID YOU KNOW? UCLA LEGEND LEW ALCINDOR CHANGED HIS NAME TO KAREEM ABDUL-JABBAR ONE DAY AFTER WINNING THE NBA TITLE IN 1971

Why do umpires point when calling a strike?

Umpires began using hand signals more than 100 years ago so that outfielders and fans who were too far awar to hear the ump would know what was being called. Umpires use their right arm and hand to indicate a strike. Some umpires like to point when calling a strike. Others choose to call a strike by shaking a closed fist. When a player swings and misses, the umpire gives the strike hand signal by itself. But when the batter doesn't swing, the umpire must verbally call out the strike in addition to giving the hand signal.

DID YOU KNOW?
OUTFIELD UMPIRES ARE USED IN MAJOR LEAGUE BASEBALL PLAYOFFS GAMES

Why do football players wear mouth guards if they're already wearing helmets?

One reason is that the helmet's facemask doesn't cover the entire face, so a hand can get through there (just ask Steelers quarterback Ben Roethlisberger, who had his nose broken during a 2010 game). There's also the fact that a jarring hit can cause a player to bite down hard, damaging his teeth.

In recent years, some mouth guard companies have claimed that their products help prevent concussions, but there have been no scientific studies to support that claim.

Why is a football sometimes called a pigskin?

In the early days of football, and before that in rugby — from which football evolved — the ball itself was not constructed from the leather and rubber of today. Rather it was built by inflating the bladder that came from a pig. At that time, footballs were quite literally pigs' skin.

DID YOU KNOW?
FOOTBALLS WERE MADE LONGER AND SKINNIER IN 1934 TO HELP QUARTERBACKS GRIP THE BALL

Why are women's lacrosse sticks different than men's?

Women's lacrosse is a much different sport than men's field lacrosse. The basics are the same: Players carry the ball in a stick and shoot at a net. But while the women's game has largely stayed true to the roots of the sport, the men's game now allows body-checking, which makes the game a lot more physical.

The sticks in men's lacrosse have much deeper pockets and are usually made from synthetic mesh strings, which allows players more control when passing or getting hit. Men's defense sticks are also longer, creating another obstacle to fight through.

In women's lacrosse, the sticks are all the same approximate length and the pockets are much shallower. They're also traditionally strung with leather. Stick-handling and shooting are very challenging with the shallower pocket. Basically, skill is much more important than strength in the women's game.

Why is there a semi-circle at the top of the penalty area in soccer?

That semi-circle is known as the penalty arc. It's not considered part of the penalty area (18-yard box) where penalty kicks take place.

The penalty arc's only job is to keep players from both teams away from the person taking the penalty kick. To make this fair for all the players trying to get in position for a potential rebound, every point on that arc is exactly 10 yards from the penalty mark — where the penalty kick is lined up.

Why do some basketball players wear an arm sleeve?

In all probability, the arm sleeve is nothing more than a fashion accessory. But the first famous player to wear the arm sleeve did it to help an injury. Philadelphia 76ers star and NBA scoring champion Allen Iverson started wearing a black arm sleeve on his right arm because he thought it helped relieve the pain from elbow bursitis. A lot of players gave it a try, and since Iverson was such a trendsetter at the time, many started wearing a sleeve just to look like him.

DID YOU KNOW? SOME PLAYERS BELIEVE AN ARM SLEEVE KEEPS THEIR ARM INJURY-FREE, BUT NO SCIENTIFIC PROOF FOR THAT CLAIM EXISTS

Why do most righthanded NHL players shoot lefty and lefthanded players shoot righty?

It might surprise you to learn that the majority of players in the NHL play lefthanded (with their left hand lower on the stick and the blade to the left side). In 2006, 60 percent of NHL forwards and 70 percent of defensemen played lefthanded. How could that be when the majority of people are naturally righthanded?

There are a couple of theories that could explain it. First, there's the fact that many professional players started playing at a very young age. And when very young players start to skate, one of the first things they learn to do is hold the stick with one hand at the top to poke check. These young players use their dominant hand, which for most people is the right hand. So when it's time to start stick-handling and shooting, players simply keep the right hand at the top and place their left hand lower — thus the lefthanded grip.

There's also the fact that in Canada the majority of skaters play lefthanded, but in the U.S. the majority plays righthanded. That could be because players start younger in Canada. But it could also be because, in the U.S., baseball is a popular sport. And since most baseball players hit righty, the ones who decide to also play hockey hold the stick the same way they do a bat, righthanded.

Why is a flaming torch an iconic symbol of the Olympics?

Every four years when the Olympics are held, a torch is lit in the ancient Olympic stadium in Olympia, Elis, Greece. The flame starts its relay by touring Greece. Then it is transported (usually by plane) to the country currently hosting the Olympic games. Once there, it is carried around on foot, and by horse or camel. The last runner uses the torch to light a much larger Olympic torch that burns throughout the Games. The flame itself represents the death and rebirth of Greek heroes.

Why is Boise State's football field blue?

At first glance, it looks like Boise State football players are walking on water. It turns out it's just that the artificial turf at Bronco Stadium isn't traditional green, but rather blue in honor of the school's colors.

In 1986, Broncos Stadium needed to replace its artificial turf, which was green at the time. But athletic director Gene Bleymaier didn't like the idea of spending money to purchase a playing surface that looked the same as what was there before. So he decided on a new look: blue.

Visiting teams often claimed that the blue turf gave Boise State an unfair advantage, that it served as camouflage for the Broncos' blue jerseys. In 2011, when the team joined the Mountain West Conference, officials ruled that Boise State could not wear all blue — blue jerseys *and* blue pants — at home against conference foes. They can still wear all blue against non-conference opponents.

DID YOU KNOW? IN 2010, EASTERN WASHINGTON CHANGED THE COLOR OF THEIR TURF TO RED

Why are lefthanded pitchers called southpaws?

It's a term that originated with baseball. In the 19th century, most baseball diamonds were built so the batter was facing east. That way, the setting sun wouldn't be in the batter's eyes. If you picture the diamond like a compass, third base would be north and first base would be south. A pitcher's left arm would be on the south side. Paw is simply a slang word for hand. Thus, a lefty became known as a southpaw.

Why do they call that swimming stroke the butterfly?

Swimmers move their arms during this difficult stroke a lot like the way butterflies move through the air.

The butterfly stroke evolved from the breaststroke. The breaststroke is a slower swimming stroke than any other because both the arms and legs finish their motions at the same time in the water, which slows a swimmer's momentum.

In an attempt to speed up the stroke, University of Iowa swim coach David Armbruster figured out a way to modify the breaststroke in 1934. He had swimmers finish their arm motions out of the water. This improved speed.

The next year, one of his swimmers, Jack Sieg, developed the dolphin kick. The two men put these new motions together to create the butterfly stroke. This way of swimming the breaststroke became its own legal — and separate — stroke in the 1950s.

63

Why is the NCAA men's basketball tournament referred to as March Madness?

A college basketball tournament wasn't the original "March Madness." That was Illinois' high school basketball tournament. In 1939, Henry V. Porter, assistant executive secretary of the Illinois High School Association, referred to the state-wide championship tournament as March Madness in an *IHSA* magazine article. The term only referred to the Illinois high school tournament until 1982. That's when TV announcer Brent Musburger, who was once a sports writer in Chicago, Illinois, referred to the NCAA tournament as March Madness during a CBS broadcast.

Why are there designated hitters only in the American League?

The idea of a designated hitter has been around since the 1890s. In the late 1920s, National League president John Heydler tried to get his league to add a 10th position to the batting order — the designated hitter — in order to speed up games. He nearly persuaded clubs to try the idea during spring training in 1929. But ultimately, that attempt failed.

Fast-forward 40 years to 1969. By this time, both leagues were looking at new ways to help hitters. The year before, a pitcher had won 31 games, and another pitcher had posted an earned run average (ERA) of only 1.12. So Major League Baseball lowered the pitcher's mound from 15 to 10 inches and made the strike zone smaller.

Each league was also considering the designated hitter. They planned to test it during spring training in 1969, but most National League teams didn't actually participate, so MLB dropped the issue. On January 11, 1973, the owners of the American League teams voted to try out the designated hitter rule for three years. It was later adopted by that league full-time and has been in use ever since. The National League never embraced the concept.

DID YOU KNOW?
DAVID ORTIZ SET A RECORD WHEN HE HIT HIS 270TH CAREER HOME RUN AS A DESIGNATED HITTER ON SEPTEMBER 15, 2009

Why is it called the slalom when skiers ski around tightly spaced poles?

The word slalom combines two Norwegian words. *Sla* indicates "a small hill or slope." And *lam* means "to track." Together they mean following a track down a slope. Slalom skiers do just this when they compete in the event. Men weave among 55 to 75 alternating red and blue poles as they race down a mountain. Women navigate 40 to 60 poles. The skier with the fastest time wins, but if a skier misses even a single pole, he or she is disqualified from the event.

QUIZ TIME

Has reading this section turned you into an All-Star sports fan? Find an adult who knows a lot about sports and see if he or she knows as much as you!

1 In 1975, a group of skaters from California started going to which state to skateboard in giant water pipes being built to divert water from the Colorado River?

(**a**) Arizona
(**b**) Colorado
(**c**) Nevada
(**d**) Utah

Your answer: ◯
Adult's answer: ◯

2 What does the H inside the C in the Montreal Canadiens logo stand for?

(**a**) Habitants
(**b**) Heat
(**c**) Hockey
(**d**) Home

Your answer: ◯
Adult's answer: ◯

3 What was sprinter Usain Bolt's time when he set a world record in the 100 meters in 2009?

(**a**) 9.58 seconds
(**b**) 11.17 seconds
(**c**) 12.86 seconds
(**d**) 14.03 seconds

Your answer: ◯
Adult's answer: ◯

4 The Heisman Trophy is modeled after Ed Smith, a running back who played from 1933 to '35. Which college team did Smith play for?

(**a**) New York University
(**b**) Notre Dame
(**c**) Ohio State
(**d**) Stanford

Your answer: ◯
Adult's answer: ◯

5 The term March Madness first referred to which state's high school basketball tournament?

(**a**) Illinois
(**b**) Indiana
(**c**) Iowa
(**d**) Minnesota

Your answer: ◯
Adult's answer: ◯

6 What was the name of the Greek soldier who inspired the marathon by supposedly running about 25 miles to Athens to deliver news of the Greeks' successful surprise attack on the Persians in 490 B.C.?

(a) Hippocrates
(b) Marathonicus
(c) Pheidippides
(d) Spartacus

Your answer: ○
Adult's answer: ○

7 The first Olympics featured only one event, called a stadion. What kind of an event was it?

(a) cycling
(b) jumping
(c) running
(d) wrestling

Your answer: ○
Adult's answer: ○

8 How many NASCAR crew members are allowed onto pit lane during a stop?

(a) 3
(b) 7
(c) 11
(d) 15

Your answer: ○
Adult's answer: ○

9 Women weave among how many alternating poles as they race against the clock in a slalom event?

(a) 20 to 40
(b) 40 to 60
(c) 60 to 80
(d) 80 to 100

Your answer: ○
Adult's answer: ○

10 In which year did American League team owners vote to first try out the designated hitter rule?

(a) 1963
(b) 1973
(c) 1983
(d) 1993

Your answer: ○
Adult's answer: ○

ANSWERS:

(1 = a) (2 = c) (3 = a) (4 = a) (5 = a) (6 = c) (7 = c) (8 = b) (9 = b) (10 = b)

Your Total Score: ○ | **Adult's Total Score:** ○

LEVEL 1 2 ③ 4

MVP QUESTIONS

Why do sports teams have mascots?

The tradition of having mascots dates back to at least the Civil War. Many army regiments then had live animals traveling with them. One of them was Old Abe, the bald eagle named after Abraham Lincoln. She accompanied the 8th Wisconsin regiment to dozens of battles, and became famous for a fierce battle cry. Sallie, a bull terrier, started traveling with the 11th Pennsylvania Volunteer Infantry when she was still a puppy. She was known for standing over wounded soldiers on the battlefield. These animals helped lift their infantries' spirits during battles, just like today's mascots help lift the spirits of fans and some athletes during games.

DID YOU KNOW?
BEFORE BECOMING A PADRES MASCOT, THE SAN DIEGO CHICKEN GAVE EASTER EGGS TO CHILDREN AT THE SAN DIEGO ZOO

Why is zero called 'love' in tennis?

One possibility is that a zero is shaped like an egg. The French word for egg is *"l'oeuf,"* which sounds a lot like "love" in English.

Another possibility is the 17th-century saying "play for love." This meant competing in tennis or other activities simply for the joy of it (not money). They were playing for "nothing." And everybody knows that nothing equals zero. Thus, zero equals love.

DID YOU KNOW?

WHEN A TENNIS PLAYER HITS THE BALL BACK ACROSS THE NET BEFORE THE BALL TOUCHES THE GROUND IT'S CALLED A VOLLEY

Why do referees wear striped shirts?

In 1920, Dr. Lloyd Olds was refereeing a Michigan State-Arizona football game. Olds was wearing an all-white dress shirt, typical of most officials at the time. Unfortunately, the shirt looked a lot like Arizona's all-white uniforms. The Arizona players thought so too, as on numerous occasions they mistook Olds for a teammate.

Olds decided refs needed attire that would look different no matter what the teams wore. He and a friend designed a black-and-white striped shirt, which Olds first wore during high school basketball championships in 1921. The look made sense and caught on across sports.

Why are there no lefthanded-throwing infielders aside from first basemen?

Lefties are a poor fit for the infield because most throws go to first base. And for a lefty to field the ball facing home plate and then get the ball to first base, he would be forced to awkwardly rotate his body to make the throw.

That's not to say there have never been lefthanders at second base, shortstop or third. Since 1900, there have been a handful at each position. In the early part of the century, Hal Chase of the Yankees often played second base and sometimes filled in at shortstop. Around that time, Hall of Famer "Wee" Willie Keeler played some second base and third base.

More recently, former Yankees star Don Mattingly (a lefthanded first baseman) went across the diamond. In 1986, Mattingly made two starts and played three total games at third base. He recorded 11 assists, started two double plays, and made just one error.

Why does the Zamboni come out onto the ice between periods of a hockey game?

Over the course of a game, skating really tears up the ice. That's where the Zamboni comes in.

Frank Zamboni invented the machine in 1949. A Zamboni resurfaces the ice so that it's as good as new. It shaves off a top layer of the ice, lifts it, and collects it in a snow tank. Then another part of the Zamboni washes the ice to clean it. Finally, it puts down a layer of water, which freezes to create the new ice surface for the next period of play.

Why is Philadelphia's basketball team called the 76ers?

The 76ers began as the Syracuse Nationals, playing in the state of New York from 1949 to '63. When the Nationals relocated to Philadelphia in 1963, they were looking for a new team name. The franchise held a contest for fans, and a man named Walter Stalberg beat out over 4,000 other contestants when he came up with 76ers in honor of 1776. That's the year the country's founding fathers signed the Declaration of Independence in Philadelphia. Stalberg explained: "No athletic team has ever paid tribute to the gallant men who forged this country's independence, and certainly Philadelphia, Shrine of Liberty, should do so."

DID YOU KNOW? THE WARRIORS WERE PHILLY'S FIRST BASKETBALL FRANCHISE, BUT THE CITY LOST THE TEAM TO NORTHERN CALIFORNIA IN 1962

Why does the lacrosse team that last touched a ball that goes out of bounds sometimes get to maintain possession?

This one can be awfully confusing to anyone who is new to lacrosse. If the ball goes out of bounds, the other team is awarded possession, just like in every other sport. However, the rule is much different if the ball goes out of bounds on a missed shot.

If the official judges it to be an attempt on goal, then the ball is awarded to the player closest to the ball when it goes out of bounds. It's not just closest to the end line, but closest to where the ball actually crossed the line. Reaching a stick out to get closer doesn't count. The officials judge it on the position of a player's body.

Why are the Chicago Cubs cursed?

According to legend, it is all because of a goat. In 1945, the Cubs were up in the World Series, two games to one, over the Detroit Tigers. Hoping to bring Chicago good luck, local tavern owner William "Billy Goat" Sianis bought two tickets for Game 4, one for himself and one for his goat. When the ushers wouldn't let the goat into the park, Sianis asked Cubs owner P.K. Wrigley to allow it. Wrigley said Sianis could come in, but the goat couldn't because it smelled terrible.

Upset, Sianis supposedly said "The Cubs ain't gonna win no more. The Cubs will never win a World Series so long as the goat is not allowed in Wrigley Field." The Cubs lost Game 4, and the Series. Sianis later sent a telegram to Wrigley that read "Who stinks now?" The Cubs haven't won or even been to a World Series since.

Why are Syracuse's athletic teams called the Orange?

Syracuse came a long way to become the Orange. Their original school colors were pink and green! The University adopted orange as the official school color in 1890; it appealed to students since no other university used orange as their main color. Until 2004, Syracuse's teams were known as the Orangemen and Orangewomen. But in '04, it was shortened to Orange so that all school teams could use the same name.

Syracuse's first mascot, adopted in 1931, was a Native American called the Saltine Warrior. But he was dropped in 1978 because the school felt that the mascot had become offensive to Native Americans.

DID YOU KNOW?
SYRACUSE'S CHEERLEADERS GAVE THEIR MASCOT THE NAME "OTTO"

Why is there a shot clock in basketball?

One of basketball's biggest appeals is that the games are high scoring. But that wasn't always the case. In the early 1950s, teams would get a lead in the first half, then stall for minutes at a time in the second half. On November 22, 1950, the Fort Wayne Pistons beat the Minneapolis Lakers by one point. A thrilling victory? Not exactly. The final score was 19-18, the lowest-scoring game in NBA history.

Something had to be done. Syracuse Nationals owner Danny Biasone had an idea. He figured 120 shots were taken during an average game, which is 2,880 seconds long; 2,880 divided by 120 is 24. The NBA adopted the 24-second shot clock in 1954, which many believe saved the struggling league.

Why are yellow and red cards used to indicate serious fouls in soccer?

During the 1966 World Cup in England, there was a particularly chippy quarterfinal match between the host country and Argentina. Newspaper stories said two of England's players, brothers Bobby and Jack Charlton, had been "booked" by the referee. That means they had committed serious fouls, but were not ejected. However, the English team had no idea it had happened. Former referee Ken Aston was in charge of the officials at that year's tournament. He decided there had to be a clearer way of communicating bookings. Inspired by a traffic light, (yellow means caution, red means stop) Aston introduced a card system that every player in the world could understand. A yellow card is a warning, a red card an ejection.

DID YOU KNOW?
THE 2010 WORLD CUP FINAL HAD 14 YELLOW CARDS, WHICH WAS MORE THAN TWICE AS MANY AS ANY PREVIOUS WORLD CUP FINAL

Why are speed skating skates different from figure skates and hockey skates?

The different kinds of activities that people perform on an ice rink require different types of skates. Speed skaters rely on long, thin blades with a flat bottom to help them generate the high speed they need to compete for the win. The longer the blade, the faster it is possible to go. Blades on these skates are usually between 12 and 18 inches long. Figure skaters have shorter, thicker blades, but their skates have another feature. At the front of the blade is the toe pick. This jagged edge allows figure skaters to execute the elaborate footwork and jumps necessary to impress the judges watching them. Hockey players use a short, light blade. Like figure skates, the blades on hockey skates are hollowed out on the bottom. This creates two sharp edges, which help hockey players make the fast cuts and turns essential for the fast changes in direction.

DID YOU KNOW?

THE FIRST SKATES WERE CONSTRUCTED BY ATTACHING ANIMAL BONES TO THE FEET WITH LEATHER STRAPS

Why does my soccer team eat orange slices at halftime?

During a soccer halftime, parents and team trainers across the country serve orange slices to children because the fruit appears to provide quick energy that kids can use to compete during the rest of the match. The sugar, called fructose, found in fruits such as oranges does indeed cause a spike in blood sugar levels. However, since fructose also slows digestion in the stomach, athletes who eat these orange slices could actually end up a little slower and have less energy to start the second half.

Why is a ball fair if it hits the foul pole?

Think of it this way: The foul pole is just an extension of the foul line. And a ball that hits the white foul line is fair. But why is the foul line fair? For that you have to go back to the early days of baseball.

Originally, the foul lines weren't in the base paths like they are now. They were meant to keep spectators off the field, and the lines were considered foul territory (which is why they were called foul lines). The problem was that first and third base were actually outside the lines. In 1886, first and third base were moved so that they were inside the lines, in fair territory. A batted ball touching one of those bases was considered fair.

Fast-forward to 1900. That's the year home plate was changed from a square shape to the pentagon shape of today. The fifth point on home plate (where it comes together like a roof on a house) is evened up so that the foul lines on either side start at that point and are drawn out to touch first and third base. Those bases are in fair territory. Thus, the foul lines were now in fair territory too!

Why do hockey players put tape on their stick blades?

In the early 1900s, players taped the blade of their stick for a very practical reason: to keep it from splintering and cracking. Sticks were made out of wood and players expected to use them for years, so they used tape to take care of them.

New wooden sticks became more durable over the years, and most of today's sticks are made out of fiberglass, which very rarely cracks. So why is tape still used? It helps players control the puck, especially when receiving passes, by adding cushioning (and a little bit of stickiness) to the blade.

Why are the St. Louis Rams in the NFC West division and the Dallas Cowboys in the NFC East even though St. Louis is farther east than Dallas?

Like most of the NFL's reasons for configuring their divisions, it has everything to do with tradition and rivalries.

When the NFL split into divisions in 1967, all of the divisions were given names that started with "C." The Cowboys were in the Capitol Division with the Eagles, Saints and, obviously, the Washington Redskins. The Saints and New York Giants flip-flopped between the Capitol and Century Divisions the next two seasons. When the league switched to the East, Central, and West division names in 1970, they kept the Cowboys in the East because they were rivals with the division's other teams.

As for the Rams, they were in Los Angeles when the league originally split into divisions. It wasn't until 1995 that they moved to St. Louis. When the league switched to the current eight-division alignment in 2002, the Rams stayed in the West Division, largely because of the rivalries they had with San Francisco and Arizona, but in part because the NFC had only three teams West of the Central time zone.

DID YOU KNOW?

BACK IN 2001, THE ATLANTA FALCONS, CAROLINA PANTHERS, AND NEW ORLEANS SAINTS WERE ALL IN THE NFC WEST

Why do distance runners train in high altitude?

They train in high places because there is less oxygen there. While this fact causes athletes to quickly lose their breath and burn out muscles when they first start training, over time it also changes their bodies in ways that are advantageous.

As they continue to train, athletes' bodies will produce more red blood cells to account for the lack of oxygen. Their bodies will also form more hemoglobin, which is the part of red blood cells that holds on to molecules of oxygen. The lungs get better at processing oxygen, and the blood vessels around muscles become denser, delivering more oxygen to the muscles and removing more waste from cells. This all helps the athlete perform better, especially when he or she competes at a lower elevation. This physical advantage can be lost in just a few weeks, however, so athletes often employ this tactic soon before a big competition.

DID YOU KNOW?
ELDORET, KENYA, WHICH SITS MORE THAN 7,000 FEET ABOVE SEA LEVEL, PRODUCES MANY TOP DISTANCE RUNNERS

Why are college footballs a different size and shape than professional footballs?

According to Wilson, the company that supplies footballs to the NCAA and NFL, there *is* no difference in size or shape. Individual footballs do vary slightly though. Balls can be 11 to 11½ inches long, 28 to 28½ inches in circumference and weigh 14 to 15 ounces.

Unlike pro footballs, college footballs have white lines around half of each end. This feature was added to help players see the ball under artificial lighting. In the NFL, certain balls are marked with a K and only used for kicks.

Why do catchers wear a different glove than other fielders?

Catchers have always been a little different when it comes to glove wear because they're catching the ball on almost every play.

In 1870, Cincinnati catcher Doug Allison decided he needed some padding for his injured left hand and wore a pair of buckskin mittens. The first padded catcher's mitt, more of a pillow combined with a glove, came about 10 years later — although historians debate who it was that developed the idea.

The different catcher's mitt makes perfect sense. Catching a few dozen fastballs can be tough on the hands. That's why the extra padding is needed.

DID YOU KNOW? BECAUSE KNUCKLEBALLS ARE SO HARD TO CATCH, CATCHERS WILL USE A MITT SIMILAR TO A FIRST BASEMAN'S GLOVE WHEN CATCHING KNUCKLEBALL PITCHERS

Why don't the Cleveland Browns have a logo on their helmet?

Cleveland Browns fans actually consider the lack of a design to *be* their logo. The idea is that nothing is more important than the team, or than the principles originally drilled into the squad by legendary coach Paul Brown, for whom the team is named.

DID YOU KNOW?
THE MAIN COLOR ON THE CLEVELAND HELMET IS BURNT ORANGE

Why are tennis balls fuzzy?

Tennis balls are fuzzy so they will create friction. This slows the ball down and makes it easier to control in the small space of a tennis court. It also causes the ball to roll on a racket or the surface of the court instead of slide along it. Players are better able to predict what the ball will do. A fuzzy ball also grabs the court more than a smooth one would. This means it will take on some characteristics of the playing court. With a smooth ball, tennis played on grass, clay, or concrete would be virtually the same experience.

DID YOU KNOW?
THE FUZZY OUTSIDE OF A TENNIS BALL IS MADE OF FELT

Why do curling stones have handles on them?

If you've ever seen curling at the winter Olympics (it's the sport that's like shuffleboard, but with brooms), you might think it's a really easy sport. But it's much tougher than it looks, especially the art of curving, or curling, a stone.

That's where the handle comes in. The thrower needs to put just the right rotation on the stone. This rotation is used to knock another stone off the playing surface (called a sheet) at the correct angle; perhaps a team wants to knock an opponent's stone out, but not knock that stone into one of their own. Or sometimes the stone is going to be curled around another stone that's acting as an obstacle (called a guard).

Along with the thrower's rotation, the sweepers also help guide the stone to where the team wants it. Sweeping heats up the ice and reduces friction, causing the stone to travel faster and farther.

DID YOU KNOW? CURLING STONES WEIGH BETWEEN 38 AND 44 POUNDS, AND ARE TRADITIONALLY MADE OF GRANITE

Why is it called a bobsled?

If you always thought it was because a guy named Bob invented it...well, you've been wrong. Bobsledding was developed in the 1880s, both in upstate New York and in Switzerland. One of the early techniques was for the competitors to shift their weight forward and back to gain speed, causing their heads to bob up and down.

Today, bobsledding is one of the fastest sports in the Olympic games, with some sleds racing at nearly 100 miles per hour down an icy track.

The keys to success in this event are strong pushing at the start of a race and precise steering on the track during it.

In two-person bobsled, the front competitor is the pilot (or driver) and the brakeman sits in the back. In four-man, two pushers sit between the driver and brakeman. The team learns to shift their weight in unison to help the driver steer while staying at top speeds. The pushers and brakeman are unable to see the track ahead of them and have to memorize the turns.

87

Why are they the Red Sox and the White Sox, and not the Red Socks and the White Socks?

In the early 1900s, many groups wanted to simplify spelling in the English language. One of the suggestions was for everyone to start spelling the word socks with an x (sox). A few newspapers, including the *Chicago Tribune*, also preferred to use Sox because it was easier to fit in headlines. So the Chicago White Stockings were usually referred to as the White Sox in newspaper stories. Because newspapers influenced team names back then, the name soon stuck, and officially became the team's name in 1904.

The Boston team, originally known as the Boston Americans, changed their name in 1908 to the similar Red Sox to reflect their uniforms.

DID YOU KNOW?
THE CINCINNATI REDS WERE ONCE CALLED THE RED STOCKINGS

Why does the NBA use a lottery to determine the order of their draft?

The NBA is worried that teams with poor records may lose games on purpose late in a season in hopes of getting the top pick in the next draft. To combat that concern, the league started a lottery system in 1985 so that the worst team was no longer guaranteed the top pick. The New York Knicks won the first lottery after having the league's third-worst record. The Knicks used the first pick in the 1985 NBA Draft to select future Hall of Famer Patrick Ewing.

In 1990, the NBA switched to a weighted lottery system so that the worst team would have the best chance of winning that top pick, but that scenario doesn't happen every time. In fact, the team with the worst record has won the lottery only three times since 1990. It has led to some serious controversies over the years, but clearly the NBA is not interested in rewarding teams that post terrible records.

Why do the Pittsburgh Steelers have a logo on only one side of their helmets?

In the 1950s, logos on football helmets were becoming more popular. The Steelers used player numbers on both sides of their gold helmets for a few years, but they didn't love the look. In 1962, Cleveland's Republic Steel suggested they use the Steelmark logo.

The team agreed to give it a try, but they weren't sure how the logo would look on their gold helmets. So equipment manager Jack Hart put the logo on only the right side of the helmets to test the new look against the old. The Steelers had been a hapless franchise to that point in history, but in 1962 they won a team-record nine games and qualified for the Playoff Bowl for the first time. The team wanted to do something special for that game, so they changed their helmet color from gold to the familiar black they wear today.

Because of the good fortune they had that season, the Steelers decided to keep the new look.

Why is a quadruple Axle so difficult?

All figure skating jumps that require four full turns are difficult to land. But two factors make the attempt at a quadruple Axle so hard that no one has ever accomplished the feat. Most skating jumps happen from a backward takeoff. However, the Axle requires a forward takeoff. This atypical approach is a challenge by itself. But it also adds distance to the jump — an extra ½ rotation for 4½ total turns. That means skaters have to build a lot of momentum to make the necessary spins while in the air. That much power is hard to control, and makes landing the jump impossible — so far.

89

Why do the Harlem Globetrotters always play against the same team?

The Globetrotters are not truly a competitive team, but rather a form of entertainment. To amuse a crowd they perform neat tricks, winning games in fabulous and interesting ways.

To remain popular, the Globetrotters play against a team they beat almost every time. From 1953 to '95, the Globetrotters won more than 13,000 games against a team called the Washington Generals, which sometimes went by other names to give the appearance of more teams. The Globetrotters' last loss came on January 5, 1971, when the Generals were known as the New Jersey Reds.

DID YOU KNOW?

IN 1959, FUTURE NBA GREAT WILT CHAMBERLAIN PLAYED WITH THE GLOBETROTTERS DURING THEIR TOUR OF THE SOVIET UNION

Why might teams use the squeeze play during games?

Squeeze plays consist of a batter bunting while one or more runners try to score. Managers sometimes try this tactic when their team needs one run to tie a game, break a tie, or increase a small lead. Executed well, a squeeze play is hard for a defense to stop. But doing it well is difficult since multiple players have to do things correctly at the same time.

There are three types of squeeze plays. During a safety squeeze, a runner on third base waits to see how the batter bunts the ball. If it is bunted well, he runs home. If the batter pulls back his bat, misses the bunt, or bunts badly, the runner retreats back to third base.

During a suicide squeeze, the runner is coming home no matter what. He takes a lead at third and sprints toward home as the pitch is delivered. If the batter misses the bunt for any reason, the defense will easily tag out the runner.

The third type of squeeze — a double squeeze — is a suicide squeeze with an extra base runner involved. Double squeezes are extremely rare. Once the pitcher begins his delivery, a runner on second base runs toward third. He rounds third base without slowing down and continues toward home plate.

DID YOU KNOW?

A FOUL BUNT THAT IS NOT CAUGHT IN THE AIR IS ALWAYS COUNTED AS A STRIKE, EVEN IF IT IS A THIRD STRIKE

Why isn't all-time hits leader Pete Rose in the Hall of Fame?

There's no doubt that Pete Rose had a Hall of Fame-caliber playing career. Known as Charlie Hustle for his all-out style of play, Rose spent 24 seasons in the big leagues. He was a 17-time All-Star and collected more career hits than any player in Major League Baseball history with 4,256. Many of Rose's artifacts have been donated to the Hall of Fame, so how does he not have a plaque there?

It's all because Rose committed one of baseball's cardinal sins: betting on games. Rose took over as manager of the Cincinnati Reds in 1984 and was later found to have wagered money on Reds games during the 1987 season. In 1989, he was banned permanently from baseball, meaning he can no longer manage and he is ineligible for the Hall of Fame. For 18 years, Rose denied the gambling allegations. In 2007, he finally confessed that the accusations were true.

DID YOU KNOW? PETE ROSE IS ALSO THE ALL-TIME MAJOR LEAGUE LEADER IN CAREER OUTS WITH 10,328

Why are shooting and skiing the two sports that make up the biathlon?

The biathlon was first contested at the 1924 Winter Olympics, but did not become an official part of the Games until 1960. So how did shooting and cross country skiing, two very different activities, end up in the same event?

The biathlon started in the 1860s as a training activity for Norwegian soldiers to help improve national defense. It steadily evolved into a competition, combining the endurance of cross country skiing with the concentration and precision of riflery. Today, there are competitions of varying lengths and even team relay races. Typically, a biathlete has to hit five targets in the shooting portion. For each missed target, there is a penalty, such as skiing a penalty loop, added time, or a limited extra cartridge. The winner is the athlete or relay team with the fastest total time.

DID YOU KNOW?
DESPITE INVENTING THE SPORT, NORWAY IS SECOND IN THE ALL-TIME BIATHLON OLYMPIC MEDAL COUNT BEHIND GERMANY

Why do some teams have grass while others use an artificial surface?

Individual teams are allowed to use a surface that they think will provide a competitive edge. Teams with speed often use artificial turf to help them play faster against opponents. Most dome teams use turf due to the difficulty of accessing light and water.

The 1968 Houston Oilers, who were in the AFL at the time, were the first major pro football team to play home games on artificial turf. The Eagles became the first NFL team to play on artificial turf after it was installed at Philadelphia's Franklin Field in 1969.

AVAI

94

Why do male gymnasts use a pommel horse?

The extreme upper-body strength required to perform on the pommel horse makes it a male-only event. Women, especially teenaged women, aren't able to build the large shoulder muscles needed to support the constant motions on this equipment. The rings are a male-only event for this same reason. In contrast, men can't compare to women when it comes to balance, and so men do not compete on the balance beam.

Why might teams run a hurry-up offense?

NFL teams usually use a hurry-up offense for one of two reasons. Either they want to create favorable mismatches by making it difficult for opposing defenses to substitute players between plays, or they want to move the ball downfield fast to tie or win a game.

While trying to create mismatches, offenses will not huddle between plays. This does not necessarily mean the offense will snap the ball any faster. What it *does* mean is that defenses can't predict when the ball will be snapped. Thus the defense can't replace defensive players as often — or at all — for fear of getting a 12-men-on-the-field penalty. Sometimes an offense will already have plays in mind that they want to use on each down. Other times, an offense is trying to figure out what the defense is likely to do. The quarterback can then go with the called play or call an audible and change the play.

At the end of halftime and at the end of the game, many teams use the two-minute drill. This scheme is used to maximize the number of plays an offense can run within a short amount of time. To do this, teams often run plays that will stop the clock quickly. This means they will mostly pass, and mostly toward the sidelines. If a pass falls incomplete, the clock stops. A player stepping out of bounds before he's tackled also stops the clock.

DID YOU KNOW?
QUARTERBACK BOOMER ESIASON'S 1988 CINCINNATI BENGALS WERE THE FIRST MODERN NFL TEAM TO USE A NO-HUDDLE APPROACH AS AN OFFENSIVE PLAY STRATEGY; THE TEAM CALLED IT THEIR "ATTACK OFFENSE"

Why do they wave a checkered flag at auto races?

Checkered flags tell drivers that there are no more laps to be run. The winner is said to have "taken the checkered flag" because he or she drives past it first.

But why checkered? In his book *Origin of the Checker Flag*, automobile historian Fred Egloff ventures a guess. In the early 1900s, car manufacturers held rally races hundreds of miles long, but many of the cars broke down. So in 1906, Packard Motor Car Company worker Sidney Waldon created the checkered flag to signal where cars could stop to be repaired.

QUIZ TIME

Has reading this section turned you into an MVP sports fan? Find an adult who knows a lot about sports and see if he or she knows as much as you!

1 What was Syracuse University's original school colors?
(**a**) Black and gold
(**b**) Brown and yellow
(**c**) Pink and green
(**d**) Red, white and blue
Your answer: ◯
Adult's answer: ◯

2 According to legend, what kind of animal did Cubs fan and local tavern owner William Sianis try to bring into Wrigley Field for Game 4 of the 1945 World Series?
(**a**) a camel
(**b**) a cow
(**c**) a dog
(**d**) a goat
Your answer: ◯
Adult's answer: ◯

3 What is the ice surface called on which Olympians compete in the sport of curling?
(**a**) a mat
(**b**) a platform
(**c**) a rink
(**d**) a sheet
Your answer: ◯
Adult's answer: ◯

4 In 2001, the New Orleans Saints, Atlanta Falcons, and Carolina Panthers were all part of which NFL division?
(**a**) AFC South
(**b**) NFC Central
(**c**) NFC South
(**d**) NFC West
Your answer: ◯
Adult's answer: ◯

5 What was Boston's baseball team originally known as before the name was changed to Red Sox in 1908?
(**a**) Boston Americans
(**b**) Boston Cardinals
(**c**) Boston Patriots
(**d**) Boston Red Shoes
Your answer: ◯
Adult's answer: ◯

6 Biathlon was inspired by a training activity for soldiers in which European country's army?

(**a**) Finland

(**b**) Germany

(**c**) Norway

(**d**) Switzerland

Your answer: ◯

Adult's answer: ◯

9 Which team did the 76ers start out as before relocating to Philadelphia in 1963?

(**a**) Buffalo Braves

(**b**) Golden State Warriors

(**c**) Syracuse Nationals

(**d**) Washington Generals

Your answer: ◯

Adult's answer: ◯

7 Which team won the first NBA lottery in 1985?

(**a**) Cleveland Cavaliers

(**b**) New York Knicks

(**c**) Orlando Magic

(**d**) Philadelphia 76ers

Your answer: ◯

Adult's answer: ◯

8 What was all-time Major League Baseball hits leader Pete Rose known as because of his all-out style of play?

(**a**) All-out Pete

(**b**) Charlie Hustle

(**c**) Persistent Pete

(**d**) Runnin' Rose

Your answer: ◯

Adult's answer: ◯

10 Which lefthanded first baseman went across the diamond in 1986 to make two starts and play three total games at third base?

(**a**) Rod Carew

(**b**) Don Mattingly

(**c**) Mark McGwire

(**d**) Eddie Murray

Your answer: ◯

Adult's answer: ◯

ANSWERS:

(1 = c) (2 = d) (3 = d) (4 = d) (5 = a) (6 = c) (7 = b) (8 = b) (9 = c) (10 = b)

Your Total Score: ◯ | **Adult's Total Score:** ◯

HALL OF FAME QUESTIONS

Why do golf balls have dimples?

When a golf ball is flying through the air, two forces are holding it back — gravity and drag. Gravity is the force pulling the ball toward the ground. Drag is the force slowing the ball down during its flight. Golf ball manufacturers can't do anything about gravity. It is a constant force. But they have figured out a way to reduce drag.

Drag increases when there is more turbulence — stirred up air — behind the ball. It might seem like a golf ball with no dimples would experience an even ride through the air, and thus less drag. But that isn't the case. A smoother golf ball has a wider area of drag on the backside, slowing it down. Dimpled golf balls have a narrower area of drag on the ball's backside, helping the ball sail farther.

Why is there ivy on the walls at Wrigley Field?

It's hard to imagine now, but the home of the Chicago Cubs didn't always have Ivy on the walls. The Cubs started playing at Wrigley in 1916, and there was no ivy until 1932. Cubs owner P.K. Wrigley decided that the park had to be more beautiful. Bill Veeck Jr., who would go on to become one of baseball's best-known owners and promoters, had the idea to plant the ivy at the base of the outfield walls. More than 80 years later, Wrigley's ivy-covered walls are as famous as any player who has stepped foot on the field.

DID YOU KNOW?
WRIGLEY FIELD'S FIRST NIGHT GAME IN 1988 CAME 53 YEARS AFTER THE REDS HOSTED MLB'S FIRST GAME UNDER ARTIFICIAL LIGHTS

Why is crossing an opposing team's goal line called a touchdown?

Many of football's terms and rules are based on rugby's. In mid-19th century rugby, teams would score only by kicking the ball through the goal posts. And they got to earn that kick attempt (called a try) only if they first got a touchdown, which was placing the ball down across the opposing team's defensive end line.

So in the early days of football, a touchdown wasn't just crossing the opposing team's goal line. You had to literally place the ball on the ground in the end zone — in other words, touch it down.

Why are they the New York Jets and New York Giants if they play their home games in New Jersey?

There are two New York teams in the NFL, but neither plays in the state of New York. The Giants and Jets play home games in East Rutherford, New Jersey — seven miles from New York City.

However, both teams *did* start off playing in New York City. The Giants called Manhattan's Polo Grounds home from 1925 to '55. From there, they played at Yankee Stadium in the Bronx, at the Yale Bowl in New Haven, Connecticut, and at Shea Stadium in Queens before the move to New Jersey in 1976. The Jets played in the Polo Grounds from 1960 to '63, then at Shea Stadium, and finally in New Jersey since 1984.

It is common for NFL teams to be named after a city in which they do not play. The Washington Redskins actually play home games in Landover, Maryland. The Buffalo Bills play in nearby Orchard Park, New York. And Cowboys Stadium is in Arlington, Texas, not Dallas.

Why are baseballs dirty before the game even starts?

Brand new baseballs can be too slick to grip. Since the early days of the game, pitchers have rubbed mud on the white part of the ball (not the stitches) to improve their grip.

Today, before every game, clubhouse attendants put what's known as rubbing mud on all the brand new game balls that will be used. But baseball-rubbing mud isn't just any mud.

In the 1930s, water and dirt from the infield was used to rub up baseballs. The dirt wasn't ideal though. So, in 1938, Lena Blackburne, the third base coach for the Philadelphia Athletics, went looking for better mud. He found some along the banks of tributaries to the Delaware River near his hometown in Burlington County, New Jersey. He scooped some up and tried it out. It was perfect. It didn't smell bad, it didn't clump, and it didn't stain the ball. To this day, Lena Blackburne Baseball Rubbing Mud is still used across MLB.

DID YOU KNOW?
THE EXACT LOCATION OF THE RUBBING MUD USED TO DIRTY UP BASEBALLS IS STILL A CLOSELY KEPT SECRET

Why are NFL games traditionally played on Sunday?

In the early days of professional football, players didn't receive seven-figure signing bonuses. Not even close. There was very little money in pro football, and players held day jobs during the week. Playing on weekdays was never an option.

Some of the earliest pro football games took place on Saturdays. But few people watched them because Saturdays were when college football was played. And the college game was far more popular than the slow-growing pro game. So with Saturday out of the question, Sunday became the logical answer.

Why are some men's lacrosse sticks much longer than others?

In college lacrosse, defensemen carry longer sticks than attackmen. A defenseman's stick is 52 to 72 inches long. These sticks are effective for blocking and harassing attackmen. An attackman's stick is only 40 to 42 inches long. The shorter stick allows for more control and precise passes and shots.

Teams can have four long sticks on the field at one time. Sometimes a player with a long stick leads the attack into the offensive zone. That player is called a long-stick midfielder (or long-stick middie, or LSM). Not every team uses a LSM, and a lot of teams sub for the LSM once the ball is in the offensive end. Regardless, LSM is one of the hardest positions to play. It requires the size and toughness of a defenseman but the ball skills to spark an offensive attack.

Why do basketball players rub the soles of their sneakers?

Even on cleaned surfaces, a shoe's soles will gather a coat of dust or dirt after the player runs around for a while. When this happens, it is harder for the player to make the quick starts and stops necessary in basketball without slipping or sliding on the court. To combat that problem, many players use their hands to quickly wipe the bottom of their shoes. When players also add their own saliva to the mix, it definitely gets a bit disgusting. But in the end, it's all about gaining traction.

Why is the warm-up area called the bullpen?

No one knows for sure. Some think that bullpens were named after the holding cells used in wars and jails. The men guarding the cells were often built like bulls — big, strong, and with short tempers. Another theory is that in the 19th century, fans arriving late were put in standing-room areas in foul territory. Herded in there like cattle, the area became known as the bullpen. When that foul-ball area was later used by relief pitchers, the name stuck. Another possibility has to do with the Polo Grounds, where the New York Giants first played their games. Relief pitchers there warmed up past the left-field fence, where a nearby stockyard held real bulls.

Why are some golf clubs called 'woods' when they're all made of metal?

Because for a long time, woods were literally made of wood. Woods have always been used for greater distance. Irons, on the other hand, have always been made of metal. They're designed to put more spin on the ball.

Woods have bigger club heads and, even when they were made of hardwood, could send the ball longer distances than irons could. A big reason for that is because woods have lower loft than irons. That means the club head is more straight up and down, rather than angled. This difference propels the ball straight forward, rather than up in the air.

In 1979, the first metal woods were introduced. The club head was more stable and led to longer, straighter shots. Since the early 1980s, metal woods are what every pro has used.

DID YOU KNOW?
THE BIG BERTHA LINE OF WOODS IS NAMED AFTER GIANT CANNONS INVENTED BY GERMANY IN WORLD WAR II

Why is it called an Ollie when a skateboarder and board leap into the air?

A teenager named Alan Gelfand invented this trick at Skateboard USA in Hollywood, Florida, in 1976. His friends then attached his nickname, Ollie, to the move.

An Ollie is a way to jump over an obstacle while remaining on the skateboard. While moving forward, the rider pushes down on the tail of the board with the back foot while bending the knees to jump up and forward. The front foot slides forward on the board, rising as the board goes up. Once over the obstacle, the rider pushes both feet down suddenly to bring the board back to the ground evenly.

Why are drop kicks so rarely attempted in football games?

A drop kick is an alternative to the traditional place kick. Instead of a holder setting up the ball, the kicker can bounce it off the ground and then boot it through the uprights.

The main reason you don't see it much in football anymore is that it's not easy to do successfully. In the early days of football, the ball was more round, so it was easier to bounce in a consistent way. Because the shape of a modern football is oblong, the bounce on a drop kick can be terribly unpredictable. There have also been rule changes over the years that made the drop kick riskier; kickers didn't always have to attempt their kick from behind the line of scrimmage like they do today.

Why do the Oakland A's have an elephant on their uniform?

The name Athletics isn't much of a team identity. That name comes from the fact that the franchise was founded in 1901 as the Philadelphia Athletics baseball club. As for the elephant, it originated from their rivalry with the New York Giants. Giants manager John McGraw called the A's the White Elephants when they were starting out. A white elephant is a saying for something a person is stuck with but doesn't want. McGraw wanted the A's and the rest of the newly formed American League to be wiped out.

But A's manager Connie Mack and co-owner Benjamin Shibe decided to embrace McGraw's comments as a joke. So they adopted the white elephant as the team's symbol. Considering Mack won five World Series in his 50 years managing the A's, he seems to have gotten the last laugh.

Why is baseball's top award for pitching called the Cy Young Award?

The award is named after Hall of Fame pitcher Cy Young. In 1956, commissioner Ford Frick wanted to create a pitchers-only award. He named the award after Young as a way to honor the all-time great, who had passed away in 1955.

Young, a righthander who pitched for numerous teams from 1890 to 1911, is still baseball's all-time leader in wins (511), games started (815), complete games (749), and innings pitched (7,356).

Originally, the award was given to the best pitcher in all of Major League Baseball. In 1967, new commissioner William Eckert decided there would be a Cy Young Award winner in both the American League and National League.

DID YOU KNOW?
IN 2011, DETROIT TIGERS ACE JUSTIN VERLANDER BECAME ONLY THE 10TH PITCHER EVER TO WIN BOTH THE CY YOUNG AND MVP AWARDS IN THE SAME SEASON

Why do high jumpers twist and go over the bar back first?

It's called the Fosbury Flop, and it was invented by U.S. Olympic gold medalist Dick Fosbury in the 1960s.

High jumpers used to land in either a sand pit or on a very low mat, so they had to land feet first. In the 1950s, high jump competitions started using thicker mats. That meant jumpers could experiment with techniques that had them landing in different ways.

There was the Eastern cut-off style, where the jumper goes over sideways in an almost sitting position, kicking the front leg over the bar, then the back leg. And there was the straddle technique, in which the jumper goes over the bar sideways with the head facing down. But the Fosbury Flop took over when Fosbury used it to set a new Olympic record (7' 4¼") at the 1968 Olympics. Now, almost every high jumper attempts to clear the bar this way.

Why can't soccer players, except goalies, use their hands?

Simply put, that is the rule in soccer. But a few things should be clarified. Players may not use *any* part of their arm to gain an advantage. That includes forearms and biceps. Sometimes a ball hits a player's arm by accident. If the contact gives no clear advantage to the player, it is not a penalty. The distinction between the two scenarios is up to referees to decide. Like players, goalies aren't allowed to touch the ball when outside the penalty area.

Why are there nine innings in baseball?

There have been debates over who invented baseball and came up with the rules. The nine-inning rule is no different. Alexander Cartwright Jr.'s plaque at the baseball Hall of Fame credits him with establishing the nine-inning rule, along with many others. But it seems the Hall of Fame has the wrong guy.

When Cartwright was in charge of the New York Knickerbockers in 1857, there was a convention of area teams to establish rules. To that point, most games were seven innings with a minimum of seven players per team. It was Louis Fenn Wadsworth who proposed the rule of nine innings in a game and nine men on a team. That rule has been in place since.

114

Why would a player call for a fair catch?

On a punt or kickoff, the receiving team has the option of a fair catch. To signal it, the player receiving the ball on the return team "must raise one arm a full length above his head and wave it from side to side while the kick is in flight." Then, once the ball is caught, the play is automatically dead.

But why would the returning team give up a chance to gain return yards? Mostly for protection. A player catching a kick usually has his eyes on the ball, not on oncoming tacklers. That can leave him open to a big hit, which not only hurts a lot but could also lead to a fumble.

Another reason a team might prefer a fair catch is that they can then attempt a field goal freely from the spot of the catch. The kicker can't use a tee, but the opposing team isn't allowed to try and block it either. A free kick is rarely attempted after a fair catch because it makes sense only on the final play of a half, and from a makeable distance.

DID YOU KNOW?
IN 2010, DeSEAN JACKSON OF THE PHILADELPHIA EAGLES BECAME THE FIRST NFL PLAYER EVER TO RETURN A PUNT FOR A WINNING TOUCHDOWN ON A GAME'S FINAL PLAY

DID YOU KNOW?

A SWIMMER MUST RESURFACE WITHIN 15 METERS OF MAKING A FLIP TURN

Why do swimmers flip when they turn at the end of the pool?

At the highest levels of competitive swimming, races can be decided by a fraction of a second. So swimmers are always looking for an advantage. While training for the 1936 Olympics, backstroker Adolph Kiefer and his coach, Julian "Tex" Robertson, created one of the biggest edges in the sport's history.

The two developed the flip turn (or tumble turn), in which a swimmer gains momentum on a turn by diving under the water, flipping over, then pushing off the wall with his or her legs. Before that, freestyle and backstroke swimmers were simply getting to the wall, touching it with their hands, and then turning around and swimming the other way. The flip turn isn't used for the breaststroke or butterfly.

Why did future Hall of Fame quarterback Tom Brady not get drafted until the sixth round of the 2000 NFL Draft?

Tom Brady is a three-time Super Bowl champion and two-time NFL MVP who in 2010 became the first player ever to be unanimously voted MVP. It's hard to believe, but 198 players (including six quarterbacks) were taken before the Patriots picked Brady in the NFL draft.

Brady wasn't considered a future star for a few reasons. He played college ball at Michigan, a conservative, run-first team. So Brady didn't get many chances to show off his passing skills. He also had competition at the position.

In 1998, when Brady had finally become the Wolverines' starter as a junior, the team brought in a top-rated freshman named Drew Henson. Henson was an elite athlete who also played in the New York Yankees' minor-league system. Many Michigan fans wanted Henson to take Brady's starting spot. And sure enough, Henson often came in to play a series or two instead of Brady.

Brady's body shape and speed didn't help him either. Scouts saw a player who was skinny at just 211 pounds. In the end, too many teams failed to see the intangibles and intelligence that make Brady great.

DID YOU KNOW?

THE PATRIOTS CONSIDERED TAKING QUARTERBACK TIM RATTAY WITH THE DRAFT PICK THEY ENDED UP USING ON BRADY

Why is Shaun White's signature move, the double McTwist, so difficult?

The McTwist was invented in the early 1980s by skateboarder Mike McGill. The move is performed by spinning 540 degrees in the air (one-and-a-half rotations) with a flip in the middle. In recent years, snowboarders have adopted the trick, since the half-pipe setup, where athletes do their tricks is similar in both sports.

In early 2010, Shaun White showed off a new trick — the Double McTwist 1260. This move is so hard because instead of the normal one-and-a-half spins, a snowboarder must spin three-and-a-half times. As if that wasn't hard enough, this new move requires the rider to complete not one, but two flips at the same time. Oh, and then you still have to land the move!

Why does the Big 12 only have 10 teams, but the Big Ten has 12?

Confusing, isn't it? The Big 12 was originally the Big Eight. In 1994, they added four teams and adopted the new conference name, though the four new teams did not play athletically in the conference until 1996. The Big 12 dropped to 10 schools when Nebraska and Colorado left the conference in 2011, but they certainly couldn't change their name again since there already was a Big Ten. So they stuck with the Big 12 (in 2012, Texas A&M and Missouri left the conference, and were replaced by Texas Christian and West Virginia).

The Big Ten was known as the Western Conference before becoming known as the Big Nine after Iowa and Indiana joined Chicago, Illinois, Michigan, Minnesota, Northwestern, Purdue and Wisconsin in 1899. The conference didn't have 10 teams until Michigan re-joined in 1917 after a nine-year hiatus. But it has been a while since the Big Ten was made up of only 10 teams. Penn State joined in 1990 to raise the total to 11, but the conference decided to stick with the Big Ten name. Nebraska joined in 2011 as the conference's 12th team, but it was too late to change the name then.

DID YOU KNOW?
NEBRASKA IS THE ONLY SCHOOL TO HAVE PLAYED IN BOTH THE BIG 12 AND THE BIG 10

120

Why did old-time pitchers throw spitballs?

O ld-time pitchers used to spit on the ball, cut it in some way, or modify it with mud to make it harder for the batter to hit. When a ball has something extra on it, it behaves in odd ways during its approach to home plate. It may spin suddenly or dip sharply. Any of these atypical movements change its trajectory, which can fool a batter and lead to a strike.

A rule banning spitballs was formed in 1920. In August of that year, Carl Mays of the New York Yankees threw a spitball that hit the Cleveland Indians' Ray Chapman on the head, killing Chapman.

Why is there a seventh-inning stretch?

The history of baseball is hazy, especially when it comes to some of the sport's most timeless traditions. And the seventh-inning stretch is no exception.

There are three popular theories about the origin of the stretch. One came in a letter written by Harry Wright, who was a centerfielder for the Cincinnati Red Stockings in the 1860s. He wrote that "The spectators all arise between halves of the seventh inning, extend their legs and arms and sometimes walk about. In so doing they enjoy the relief afforded by relaxation from a long posture upon hard benches."

Another theory is based on William Howard Taft, the 27th president of the United States. Taft, who weighed more than 300 pounds, was attending a Washington Senators game against the Philadelphia Athletics. Sitting in a tiny wooden seat, Taft grew restless as the game went on. Finally, in the middle of the seventh inning, he decided to stand up and stretch his legs. As a show of respect to the president, the rest of the fans stood up with him.

A third theory comes from the college ranks. Manhattan College was playing a local semi-pro team in New York in 1892. Manhattan College's Brother Jasper noticed that the students watching the game were tired of sitting still. So in the seventh inning, Jasper called timeout and told all the fans to stand up and stretch.

DID YOU KNOW? IN AN EXTRA-INNING BASEBALL GAME, FANS WOULD STRETCH IN THE 14TH, 21ST, AND 28TH INNINGS

Why don't any NFL quarterbacks wear a uniform number higher than 19?

The NFL has very firm rules when it comes to uniform numbers. In 1952, the league started requiring offensive linemen to wear numbers between 50 and 79. That would make it easier for officials to determine which offensive players were ineligible receivers (the five offensive linemen).

By 1973, the league adopted an even stricter system that would make it easier for officials, coaches, and fans to tell what position each man played. Offensively, quarterbacks were allowed to wear a number between 1 and 19, running backs a number between 20 and 49, and wide receivers and tight ends a number between 10 and 19, or between 80 and 89.

Why are the rings the symbol of the Olympics?

Olympic games founder Baron Pierre de Coubertin developed the Olympics' ring symbol, which shows five intersecting rings. He probably got the idea when he was president of the group that represented France in the International Olympics Committee. That group had been formed from two earlier units, and their logo was two connected rings.

The five rings symbolize the different world regions that participated in the modern Olympics when they began in 1896. Those regions are Africa, the Americas, Asia, Europe, and Oceania.

DID YOU KNOW?
THE FLAG OF EVERY NATION IN THE WORLD HAS AT LEAST ONE OF THE FIVE OLYMPIC RING COLORS IN IT

123

QUIZ TIME

Has reading this section turned you into a Hall of Fame sports fan? Find an adult who knows a lot about sports and see if he or she knows as much as you!

1 The Oakland A's moved from Philadelphia to which city before landing in Oakland?
(a) Atlanta
(b) Kansas City
(c) Milwaukee
(d) New York
Your answer: ○
Adult's answer: ○

2 What is the name of the method in which a high jumper goes over the bar back first?
(a) Backflip Bernie
(b) Fosbury Flop
(c) Junebug Jump
(d) Praying Mantis
Your answer: ○
Adult's answer: ○

3 What is the name of the trick that a teenager named Alan Gelfand invented in 1976 at Skateboard USA in Hollywood, Florida?
(a) Boneless
(b) Casper
(c) Impossible
(d) Ollie
Your answer: ○
Adult's answer: ○

4 How many degrees do you have to spin in the air in order to successfully land snowboarder Shaun White's signature double McTwist?
(a) 360 degrees
(b) 540 degrees
(c) 720 degrees
(d) 1260 degrees
Your answer: ○
Adult's answer: ○

5 Which team joined the Big Ten in 1990 to the become the conference's 11th team?
(a) Michigan
(b) Nebraska
(c) Penn State
(d) Wisconsin
Your answer: ○
Adult's answer: ○

6 Philadelphia Athletics coach Len Blackburne rubbed up baseballs with mud he found near his hometown in which state?

(a) Delaware
(b) Missississpi
(c) New Jersey
(d) Pennsylvania
Your answer: ◯
Adult's answer: ◯

7 How many innings were most baseball games before the rule of nine innings in a game was proposed in 1857?

(a) 5 innings
(b) 6 innings
(c) 7 innings
(d) 8 innings
Your answer: ◯
Adult's answer: ◯

8 What type of pitch is no longer legal in today's MLB?

(a) knuckleball
(b) screwball
(c) slider
(d) spitball
Your answer: ◯
Adult's answer: ◯

9 What is the highest uniform number an NFL quarterback will wear?

(a) 17
(b) 19
(c) 29
(d) 39
Your answer: ◯
Adult's answer: ◯

10 Which former United States president is believed to have helped establish the seventh-inning stretch at baseball games?

(a) Franklin Delano Roosevelt
(b) Theodore Roosevelt
(c) William Howard Taft
(d) George Washington
Your answer: ◯
Adult's answer: ◯

ANSWERS:

(1 = b) (2 = b) (3 = d) (4 = d) (5 = c) (6 = c) (7 = c) (8 = b) (9 = d) (10 = c)

Your Total Score: ◯ | **Adult's Total Score:** ◯

Index of players, teams, and events

A

Abdul-Jabbar, Kareem, 56
Adams, Doc 19
Allison, Doug, 83
Arizona
  Cardinals, 81
  Wildcats, 71
Arizona Wildcats, 71
Armbruster, David, 63
Atlanta
  Braves, 35
  Falcons, 81

B

Baker, Dusty 12
Beckham, David, 47
Boise State Broncos, 18, 62
Bolt, Usain, 48
Boston Red Sox, 22, 54, 88
Brady, Tom, 23, 117
Brett, George, 22
Brooklyn Dodgers, 35

C

Caray, Harry, 53
Carolina Panthers, 81
Chamberlain, Wilt, 90
Chapman, Ray, 121
Chase, Hal, 72
Chicago
  Blackhawks, 27
  Bulls, 20
  Cubs, 53, 76, 101
  White Sox, 53, 88
Christophe, Eugene, 50
Cincinnati
  Bengals, 96
  Red Stockings, 122
  Reds, 43, 83, 88, 92

Cleveland
  Browns, 84
  Cavaliers, 20
  Indians, 121
Colorado Buffaloes, 120
Cox, Bobby, 35
Crosby, Sidney, 26

D

Dallas Cowboys, 28,81
Detroit
  Lions, 28
  Tigers, 28, 76, 111
Duke Blue Devils, 56
Dungy, Tony, 42

E

Eastern Washington Eagles, 62
Esiason, Boomer, 96
Ewing, Patrick, 88

F

Farkas, Andy, 11
Florida Gators, 56
Flutie, Doug, 109
Fort Wayne Pistons, 77
Fosbury, Dick, 113
French Open, 21

G

Georgetown Hoyas, 30
Georgia Bulldogs, 13
Golden State Warriors, 73
Green Bay Packers, 18
Gretzky, Wayne, 27
Gwynn, Tony, 22

H

Halladay, Roy 6
Harlem Globetrotters, 90
Hawk, Tony, 108
Hayes, Woody, 13
Heisman, John, 52
Henson, Drew, 117
Houston Oilers, 93

I

Illinois Fighting Illini, 120
Indiana Hoosiers, 120
Iowa Hawkeyes, 120
Iverson, Allen, 59

J

Jackson, DeSean, 115
James, LeBron, 20, 30
Johnson, Magic, 5
Jordan, Michael 20

K

Kaka, 5
Kaleta, Alex, 27
Kansas City Royals, 22
Keeler, Willie, 72
Keflezighi, Meb, 40
Kiefer, Adolph, 116

L

Los Angeles Lakers, 32

M

Mack, Connie, 35, 110
Malone, Moses, 5
Manhattan Jaspers, 122

CREDITS

Front Cover: Illustration by MMJ Studio / AA Reps Inc.
Back Cover: Annmarie Avila (football); Robert Beck (Clayton Kershaw); David E. Klutho (Syracuse mascot); John W. McDonough (Kobe Bryant)
Page 3: John Biever (football players); Damian Strohmeyer (David Ortiz); Heinz Kluetmeier (figure skater); Michael Zagaris/MLB Photos via Getty Images (A's mascot)
Page 4: Annmarie Avila
Page 5: Angel Martinez/Real Madrid via Getty Images (Kaká); John W. McDonough (Paul Millsap)
Page 6: Al Tielemans
Page 7: Robert Beck (Rory McIlroy); John Biever (Notre Dame)
Pages 8-9: Robert Beck
Page 10: Bill Frakes
Page 11: Al Tielemans (Hannah Kearney); Simon Bruty (Mark Sanchez)
Page 12: Chuck Solomon
Page 13: Robert Beck
Page 14: Heinz Kluetmeier
Page 15: Victor Decolongon/Getty Images (soccer); David E. Klutho (Jimmy Howard)
Pages 16-17: Heinz Kluetmeier
Page 18: Robert Beck (Boise State); Damian Strohmeyer (Clay Matthews)
Page 19: Bill Frakes (basketball); Chuck Solomon (Derek Jeter)
Page 20: Heinz Kluetmeier
Page 21: Chris Graythen/Getty Images (Tony Stewart); Heinz Kluetmeier (Rafael Nadal)
Page 22: AP
Page 23: Al Tielemans
Page 24: Damian Strohmeyer
Page 25: Julian Finney/Getty Images for DAGOC (bowling); Damian Strohmeyer (Clint Dempsey)
Pages 26-27: Fred Vulch/Sports Illustrated/Getty Images
Page 28: John Biever
Page 29: L Redkoles/Getty Images
Page 30: Sports Illustrated
Page 31: David E. Klutho (Roberto Luongo); Ryan McVay/Getty Images (archery)
Page 32: Bob Martin (Nastia Liukin); John W. McDonough (Kobe Bryant)
Page 33: Peter Read Miller (coin toss); Chuck Solomon (baseball bats)
Page 34: John W. McDonough
Page 35: Robert Beck
Page 36: Simon Bruty
Page 37: Ryan McVay/Getty Images
Page 38: David E. Klutho
Page 39: Peter Read Miller (Olympics);

Robert Beck (Giants mascot)
Page 40: Bob Levey/Getty Images
Page 41: Simon Bruty
Page 42: Al Tielemans
Page 43: Tyler Barrick/Getty Images for NASCAR (pit stop); Chuck Solomon (Joey Votto)
Pages 44-45: Janos Schmidt/ITU via Getty Images
Page 46: Chuck Solomon
Page 47: John W. McDonough (David Beckham); John Biever (E'Twaun Moore)
Page 48: Simon Bruty (football field); Bob Martin (Usain Bolt)
Page 49: Doug Pensinger/Getty Images (Shuttlecock); George Doyle/Getty Images (outfield wall)
Page 50: Michael Steele/Getty Images
Page 51: Jordin Althaus/WireImage
Page 52: Damian Strohmeyer (Andrei Kostitsyn); Manny Millan (Heisman Trophy)
Page 53: Vincent Laforet/AFP/Getty Images
Pages 54-55: Damian Strohmeyer
Page 56: Neil Leifer
Page 57: John Biever (baseball umpire); Al Tielemans (Adrian Peterson)
Page 58: Damian Strohmeyer (football); Mackenzie McCluer (women's lacrosse)
Page 59: Mike Hewitt - FIFA/FIFA via Getty Images (soccer field); Robert Beck (Paul Pierce and Ray Allen)
Page 60: David E. Klutho
Page 61: Robert Beck
Page 62: John W. McDonough
Page 63: Heinz Kluetmeier (Clayton Kershaw); Robert Beck (Olympics)
Page 64: David E. Klutho
Page 65: Damian Strohmeyer
Pages 66-67: Simon Bruty
Page 68: Bob Martin
Page 69: Tyler Barrick/Getty Images for NASCAR
Page 70: Stephen Dunn/Getty Images
Page 71: Simon Bruty (Rafael Nadal); Al Tielemans (Aaron Rodgers)
Page 72: Robert Beck
Page 73: David E. Klutho (Zamboni); Al Tielemans (Elton Brand)
Pages 74-75: Damian Strohmeyer
Page 76: AP Photo/Morry Gash (Steve Bartman); David E. Klutho (Syracuse mascot)
Page 77: John W. McDonough (shot clock); Jose Manuel Pedraza/LatinContent/Getty Images (soccer referee)
Page 78: Heinz Kluetmeier (figure skater); FotoSearch (boys soccer players)
Page 79: Doug Pensinger/Getty Images

Page 80: Damian Strohmeyer
Page 81: Rob Carr/Getty Images
Page 82: Tony Karumba/AFP/Getty Images
Page 83: Peter Read Miller (football); John Biever (baseball catcher)
Page 84: Damian Strohmeyer (Colt McCoy); Simon Bruty (tennis balls)
Page 85: Robert Beck
Pages 86-87: Bob Martin
Page 88: Damian Strohmeyer (Dustin Pedroia); Getty Images (NBA Draft board)
Page 89: Heinz Kluetmeier (Evan Lysacek); Bob Rosato (Pittsburgh Steelers)
Page 90: Simon Bruty
Page 91: John Biever
Page 92: Neil Leifer
Page 93: Bob Martin (Tora Berger); John W. McDonough (Marshall Faulk)
Pages 94-95: Al Tielemans
Page 96: Ron Vesely/Getty Images
Page 97: Chris Graythen/Getty Images
Page 98: Robert Beck
Page 99: Neil Leifer
Page 100: Chad Matthew Carlson
Page 101: John Biever (Starlin Castro); Al Tielemans (James Jones)
Pages 102-103: Jim McIsaac/Getty Images
Page 104: Mark Cunningham/MLB Photos via Getty Images
Page 105: Bill Frakes (Dan Carpenter); Damian Strohmeyer (lacrosse)
Page 106: John W. McDonough (basketball sneakers); John Biever (Atlanta Braves pitchers)
Page 107: Robert Beck
Page 108: Gregg Porteous/Newspix via Getty Images
Page 109: Al Bello/Getty Images
Page 110: Michael Zagaris/MLB Photos via Getty Images
Page 111: John Biever
Pages 112-113: Bob Martin
Page 114: Franck Fife/AFP/Getty Images (Tim Howard); Damian Strohmeyer (Fenway Park scoreboard)
Page 115: Drew Hallowell/Getty Images
Page 116: Heinz Kluetmeier
Page 117: David E. Klutho/Sports Illustrated
Pages 118-119: Robert Beck
Page 120: Heinz Kluetmeier
Page 121: Focus on Sport/Getty Images
Page 122: Doug Pensinger/Getty Images
Page 123: Robert Beck (Drew Brees); Heinz Kluetmeier (Olympics)
Page 124: Gregg Porteous/Newspix via Getty Images
Page 125: Focus on Sport/Getty Images